Cambridge
checkpoint

NEW EDITION

checkpoint
English
1

ohn Reynolds

Cambridge
checkpoint

ENDORSED BY
CAMBRIDGE
International Examinations

NEW EDITION

checkpoint
English
1

HODDER
EDUCATION
AN HACHETTE UK COMPANY

Acknowledgements

The author and publishers would like to thank Sue Bonnett for her help during the production of this book.
The publishers would like to thank the following for permission to reproduce copyright material:

Text credits

p.1 Kindle™ is a trademark of Amazon.com, Inc. or its affiliates in the United States and/or other countries, iPad is a trademark of Apple Inc., registered in the U.S. and other countries; **p.2** extract from *www.in-iceland.info*; **p.3** Bus Hub Service Pte Ltd, Singapore Zoo timetable from *www.bushub.com.sg*; **p.5** Hong Kong travel tips, website extract from *www.tourism-asia.net/query.html*; **pp.8–9** Carole Moore, Pompeii factfile from *www.thehumourwriter.com*, reproduced by permission of the author; **pp.11–12** 'Advice: How to annoy an older brother' from *http://www.ehow.com/how_4501502_annoy-older-brother. html*, reproduced by permission of Demand Media Inc; **p.13** webpage and text about hot air ballooning from *http://www.hot-air-balloon-rides.eu/hot-air-balloons-rides.php*, reproduced by permission of Montgolfiere du Bocage; **pp.14–15** webpage and text about holidaying in the Vendée from *http://holidays-in-vendee.com*, reproduced by permission of Martin Holmes, Accord Services; **pp.16–18** webpage and text, Campsite les Genêts; **pp.25–6** Steven Gerrard, extract from *Gerrard: My Autobiography* (Bantam Press, 2006), reproduced by permission of The Random House Group Ltd; **pp.27–9** Helen Forrester, extract from *Liverpool Miss* (HarperCollins, 2009), copyright © Jamunadevi Bhatia 1974, reproduced by permission of Sheil Land Associates Ltd; **pp.31–2** Amryl Johnson, extract from *Sequins for a Ragged Hem* (Virago, 1988); **p.34** Mamie Gene Cole, 'I Am The Child'; **p.35** Carol Ann Duffy, 'Your School' from *New and Collected Poems for Children* (Faber & Faber, 2009); **p.41** Richard Hughes, extract from A High Wind in Jamaica (1929); **p.42** Alexander McCall Smith, extract from *The No.1 Ladies' Detective Agency* (1998); **p.43** Gerald Durrell, extract from *Birds, Beasts and Relatives* (HarperCollins, 1971); **p.44** Charles Dickens, extract from *Hard Times* (1854); **p.45** Flann O'Brien, extract from *The Third Policeman* (Harper Perennial Modern Classics, 2007), copyright © Flann O'Brien, reproduced by permission of A. M. Heath & Co Ltd; **p.47** Charles Dickens, extract from *Hard Times* (1854); **p.48** Gerald Durrell, extract from *My Family and Other Animals* (Penguin Books, 1959); **pp.55–6** website article from *www.savetheorangutan.org*, reproduced by permission of BOS UK; **pp.58–61** Emma Cox, myView: 'School where pupils monkey around' from *The Sun*, 24 April 2010, reproduced by permission of News International Syndicate; **p.63** Medora Chevalier, 'Or will the Dreamer Wake?' from *http://slearthweek.wordpress.com/birth-a-poem-about-endangered-species*; **p.64** 'A Whale Song', reproduced by permission of Cheryl Kaye Tardif, author of the bestselling novel *Whale Song*, www.cherylktardif. com; **pp.66–7** Craig Kasnoff, website article on tigers from *http://tigersincrisis.com*; **pp.70–4** B. Sumangal, 'Stripes Tiger and the Boy' from *http://www. pitara.com/talespin/folktales/online.asp?story=57*, reproduced by permission of Pitara Kids Network; **pp.75–6** Rohini Chowdhury, 'Why the Sky is So High' from *A folktale from Bengal*, retold by Rohini Chowdhury, first published on *www.longlongtimeago.com*, copyright Rohini Chowdhury 2002, reproduced by permission of the author; **pp.77–8** 'The Bold Pedlar and Robin Hood'; **p.79** 'Pretty Boy Floyd' written by Woody Guthrie, published by Sanga Music, Inc./ Harmony Music Limited, Onward House, 11 Uxbridge Street, London, W8 7TQ, used with permission; **p.80** 'Plop!' from *Folk Tales from China Second Series* (Peking: Foreign Languages Press, 1959); **pp.84–5** William Golding, extract from *Lord of the Flies* (Faber & Faber, 1954); **pp.88–93** Susan A. Candela, extract from 'Polly Helps a Friend' from *http://www.eastoftheweb.com/short-stories.php*; **pp.95–6** 'The Owl and the Pussycat', written by Edward Lear (1871); **pp.97–99** Marriott Edgar, 'The Lion and Albert' from *The Lion and Albert* (Mammoth, 1980); **pp.100–104** Ellena Ashley, 'The Dragon Rock' from http://www.eastoftheweb.com/short-stories/contact.php, reproduced by permission of the author; **pp.105–109** Michael Rosen, 'Chocolate Cake' from *Quick, Let's Get Out of Here* (Andre Deutsch 1983, Puffin 2006). Text copyright © Michael Rosen, 1983 reproduced by permission of Penguin Books Ltd; **pp.113–5** Amy Tan, extract from 'Rules of the Game' from *The Joy Luck Club*, copyright © 1989 by Amy Tan, used by permission of G. P. Putnam's Sons, a division of Penguin Group (USA) Inc; **pp.116–9** Khamsing Srinawk, extract from 'The Gold-Legged Frog' from *The Politician and Other Stories*, translated by Domnern Garden (Silkworm Books, 2001), reproduced by permission of the publisher; **pp.120–2** Chinua Achebe, extract from 'Dead Men's Path' from *Girls at War and Other Stories* (Doubleday, 1973); **p.123** H.D. Carberry, 'Nature' from *Talk of the Tamarinds: An Anthology of Poetry for Secondary Schools*, edited by A. N. Forde (Hodder Murray, 1971), reproduced by permission of Dorothea Carberry; **p.124** Kamau Brathwaite, 'The Pawpaw' from *Talk of the Tamarinds: An Anthology of Poetry for Secondary Schools*, edited by A. N. Forde (Hodder Murray, 1971); **p.132** Jenny Joseph, 'Warning' from *Selected Poems* (Bloodaxe Books, 1992); **p.133** Roger McGough, 'First Day at School' from *In the Glassroom*, © Roger McGough 1976, is reprinted by permission of United Agents (www.unitedagents.co.uk) on behalf of Roger McGough; **pp.134–6** 'How They Brought the Good News from Ghent to Aix', written by Robert Browning; **p.138** Brian Patten, 'Geography Lesson' from *Juggling With Gerbils* (Puffin Books, 2000), copyright © 2000 Brian Patten, reproduced by permission of the author c/o Rogers, Coleridge & White Ltd., 20 Powis Mews, London W11 1JN; **p.139** Robert Pottle, 'Black Beard' from *http://www.robertpottle.com*, reproduced by permission of the author; **p.140** Edna St. Vincent Millay, 'The Little Ghost', © 1917, 1945 by Edna St. Vincent Millay; **p.141** Walter de la Mare, 'The Listeners' from *Collected Poems* (Faber & Faber, 1942), reproduced by permission of The Literary Trustees of Walter de la Mare and The Society of Authors as their representative.

All designated trademarks and brands are protected by their respective trademarks.

Photo credits

p.2 © jelwolf – Fotolia; **p.5** © Pavol Kmeto – Fotolia; **p.6** © Nils Jorgensen/Rex Features; **p.8** © Sailorr – Fotolia; **p.9** © Photodisc/Getty Images; **p.11** © Ulrike Preuss/Photolibrary.com; **p.13** Rundvald/http://commons.wikimedia.org/wiki/File:Les-Sables-dOlonne-le-Port (public domain); **p.14** © Gary – Fotolia; **p.24** © StraH – Fotolia; **p.25** © Mike Hewitt/Getty Images; **p.31** © Imagestate Media Partners Limited – Impact Photos/Alamy; **p.42** © Eric Isselée – Fotolia; **p.44** © The British Library Board, W.14/1110 (2), p.57 detail; **p.48** © mangostock – Fotolia; **p.55** © Stéphane Bidouze – Fotolia; **p.56** © Shariff Che'Lah – Fotolia; **pp.58, 59, 60** © Barcroft Media; **p.64** © Wolfgang Pölzer/Alamy; **p.66** t © Imagestate Media, b © WILDLIFE GmbH/Alamy; **p.67** © Photoshot Holdings Ltd/Alamy; **p.84** © The Moviestore Collection Ltd; **p.94** © The British Library Board, shelfmark I.B.55095; **p.95** © Lebrecht Music and Arts Photo Library/Alamy; **p.110** © David Gee/Alamy; **p.113** © Will Ragozzino/Getty Images; **p.120** © Ralph Orlowski/Reuters/Corbis; **p.123** © M. Timothy O'Keefe/Alamy; **p.129** © The British Library Board, Harley 1758, f.1; **p.136** © Bridgeman Art Library/SuperStock

t = top, *b* = bottom

Every effort has been made to trace all copyright holders, but if any have been inadvertently overlooked the publishers will be pleased to make the necessary arrangements at the first opportunity.

Hachette UK's policy is to use papers that are natural, renewable and recyclable products and made from wood grown in sustainable forests. The logging and manufacturing processes are expected to conform to the environmental regulations of the country of origin.

Orders: please contact Bookpoint Ltd, 130 Milton Park, Abingdon, Oxon OX14 4SB. Telephone: (44) 01235 827720. Fax: (44) 01235 400454. Lines are open 9.00–5.00, Monday to Saturday, with a 24-hour message answering service. Visit our website at www.hoddereducation.com.

© John Reynolds 2011
First published in 2011 by
Hodder Education, an Hachette UK Company,
338 Euston Road
London NW1 3BH

Impression number   5
Year   2015 2014 2013

Cover photo © PhotoAlto/Lawrence Mouton/Getty Images
Illustrations by Oxford Designers and Illustrators
Typeset in ITC Garamond Light 12pt by DC Graphic Design Limited, Swanley, Kent.
Printed in Dubai

A catalogue record for this title is available from the British Library

ISBN 978 1444 143836

Contents

Introduction

Welcome to *Cambridge Checkpoint English Student's Book 1*. This is the first of a series of three books aimed at international students in stages 7–9 who are preparing for the Cambridge Checkpoint Tests, with a view to IGCSE and beyond. This is an integrated series of books (each with an accompanying teacher's resource book), offering a varied and challenging range of English experiences and assignments. The books provide a comprehensive introduction to the skills needed to succeed in English at this stage and can be used as a main teaching resource or to complement teachers' own schemes of work and other materials.

Covering curriculum requirements

The content of *Student's Book 1* is firmly rooted in the Cambridge Secondary 1 English Curriculum Framework for stage 7 and focuses on the key areas of reading and writing along with underlying emphasis on language study, grammatical usage and punctuation. These skills are consolidated and revisited through each book in the series. Each chapter also contains suggested speaking and listening activities.

In each chapter there is a thematic link between the reading and writing sections, and the stimulus material reflects the suggestions for reading in the Cambridge framework. The stimulus material is drawn from both fiction and non-fiction texts written in English from countries throughout the world and from different periods of time. Pre-twentieth century literature is amply represented and, wherever possible, in an unabridged format. Reading exercises test straightforward fact retrieval, understanding of vocabulary and inferential and interpretative reading skills. Writing tasks allow students to write in a variety of genres (related to the different stimulus material) and provide opportunity to write both short passages and more extended, complex responses, in some cases as part of a small group project.

Structure

Each of the three books comprising the *Cambridge Checkpoint English* series is supported by a teacher's resource book which contains additional reference information, an audio CD and further suggestions for practice exercises related to each chapter in the student's book. A number of pages in the teacher's resource books have been designed for photocopying and use in the classroom.

Each book in the series is divided into eight chapters and follows a similar pattern, beginning with exemplar reading passages illustrating a particular type or genre of writing, followed by exercises to test both understanding and appreciation of what has been read. A range of writing tasks is set, usually linked to the type of writing exemplified by the reading exemplars; there are also suggested speaking and listening activities and, in most chapters, some prose passages or poems intended for general reading interest. Each chapter also contains information on different key skills (punctuation, parts of speech and their functions, vocabulary building and spelling, etc.) and exercises to reinforce these. The final chapter in each book of the series follows a slightly different format from the other seven as it introduces students to a more general area of English study. Although the chapters in each book have been planned so that teachers can work through them progressively in chronological order if they wish, it is not an absolute requirement to approach the course in this way. The books allow for a flexible approach to teaching and the chapters can be taught in whatever order best fits with a teacher's own scheme of work.

Assessment

As mentioned in the previous section, each chapter contains a range of exercises which will allow the assessment of students' progression through the various English skills required for success at this level. *Student's Book 3* will contain a chapter containing exercises aimed at providing specific preparation for the Cambridge Checkpoint Tests although the assessment tasks which students complete throughout the different chapters will also provide cumulatively a comprehensive preparation for these tests.

Reading

Writing that gives factual information

Wherever you look, you see words to read – you don't even have to open a book or turn on your Kindle or iPad. From advertising billboards to the destination indicator boards on local buses, from direction signs at road junctions to the menu selections on display in restaurant windows, things to read are all around us. Most of us simply absorb the information without being fully aware that we are doing so.

Taking in relevant information from written texts is one of the most common and important functions that we carry out every day. When we're reading a novel or a short story we are performing quite a complex activity as we're not only following the events of the story but we're also using our imaginations to engage with the characters in the book and the settings that they find themselves in. This form of reading will be looked at more closely in later chapters. In Chapter 1, we are going to look at how writers use language to convey factual information clearly and concisely to their readers.

Read the text extract below and the others on pages 2–6 and try to identify where you would find them.

Extract 1: Key features

- Three-bedroom townhouse
- 10 m^2 living/dining room with parquet floor
- Original wooden staircase
- Good size bathroom with shower
- Fireplace in main bedroom
- Attic space – potential for further bedroom
- Cellar
- Broadband connection, electric and gas
- Close to local amenities and golf course
- TGV Station/Airport less than 30 minutes' drive

Extract 2: Geysers in Iceland

The name of all geysers in Iceland and around the world comes from the Great Geysir that erupted in the fourteenth century. This geyser used to erupt every 60 minutes until the twentieth century when it finally became dormant. But, because of the earthquakes that occurred in June 2000, the geyser reawakened and it now erupts every 8–10 hours. Another very famous geyser in Iceland is Strokkur. This one erupts every 8 minutes, throwing water and steam to a height of approximately 20 metres. Throughout the island there can be found several other smaller geysers that can be either active or dormant. They are usually found in active volcanic areas or even lands that are prone to earthquakes. The thermal springs and boiling mud pools are considered to be characteristic of geysers.

Geysers throw up jets of hot water at regular intervals.

Features of geysers

Every one of the geysers in Iceland and around the world has a powerhouse that lies deep underground. There the surface water goes through fissures and is collected in caverns. Because of the high temperature of the volcanic rock (around 200 °C) the trapped water is heated to a very high temperature. It then expands into steam, forcing its way up and out. For example, the Great Geysir's column length is 23 metres. The water erupting from this geyser used to reach a height of 60 metres, but today its maximum is only about 10 metres. Watching geysers in Iceland erupt, no matter how small they are, can be a fascinating sight for anyone. In the beginning the water starts boiling, then a bubble forms. As the steam is much lighter than the water, it forces its way out and the bubble bursts.

Extract 3: Night Safari Singapore Zoo

Singapore Attractions Express (SAEx) offers a bus shuttle service to and from the city.

For further information, call the SAEx Hotline at (65) 6753 0506.

From City

Time			Location	Pick-Up Point
6.00p.m.	7.00p.m.	8.00p.m.	Orchard Hotel	Bus stop B20 outside Delfi Orchard
6.03p.m.	7.03p.m.	8.03p.m.	DFS Galleria	Bus stop B07 outside DFS on Scotts Rd
6.05p.m.	7.05p.m.	8.05p.m.	Sheraton Towers	Outside hotel lobby
6.10p.m.	7.10p.m.	8.10p.m.	Grand Hyatt Hotel	Bus bay outside hotel on Scotts Rd
6.12p.m.	7.12p.m.	8.12p.m.	Mandarin Orchard	Bus stop B12 opposite hotel
6.15p.m.	7.15p.m.	8.15p.m.	Concorde Hotel	Taxi stand at Kramat Lane
6.20p.m.	7.20p.m.	8.20p.m.	Hotel Rendezvous	Bus stop B01 opposite hotel on Prinsep St
6.25p.m.	7.25p.m.	8.25p.m.	The verge (on Serangoon Rd)	Outside the verge on Serangoon Rd near junction of Hastings Rd (next to the 7–11 store)
6.30p.m.	7.30p.m.	8.30p.m.	The Claremont Hotel	Along Owen Rd – opposite Fortuna Hotel (near Mustafa Centre)
7.00p.m.	8.00p.m.	9.00p.m.	Night Safari	

To City

Time	Location	Pick-Up Point
9.00p.m.	Night Safari	At the bus stop outside the Singapore Zoo/Night Safari
9.30p.m.	Night Safari	At the bus stop outside the Singapore Zoo/Night Safari
10.00p.m.	Night Safari	At the bus stop outside the Singapore Zoo/Night Safari
10.30p.m.	Night Safari	At the bus stop outside the Singapore Zoo/Night Safari
11.00p.m.	Night Safari	At the bus stop outside the Singapore Zoo/Night Safari
11.30p.m.	Night Safari	At the bus stop outside the Singapore Zoo/Night Safari

Fare Type	Adult	Child
Single Trip	$4.00/trip	$2.00/trip
Daily Pass	$12.00/day (24hrs)	$6.00/day (24hrs)

For further information, call the SAEx Hotline at (65) 6753 0506 or email enquiry@bushub.com.sg or visit www.bushub.com.sg

Extract 4: Chocolate Brownies

Makes 6 large wedges

Ingredients:
200 g dark chocolate
100 g unsalted butter, softened
250 g caster sugar
4 eggs, beaten
1 tsp vanilla essence
60 g plain flour
60 g cocoa powder

Directions:

1 Preheat the oven to 165°C and grease and line a 15 cm by 15 cm square brownie tin or baking tin.
2 Break up the chocolate into small pieces in a heatproof bowl and melt it down over a pan of gently simmering water. Remove from the heat and leave to cool until needed.
3 Whisk the butter and sugar together until they are light and fluffy and then gradually beat in the eggs. Add the vanilla extract and mix well.
4 Fold in the melted chocolate mixture and then sift in the flour and cocoa.
5 When the mixture is well combined, transfer to the prepared tin and cook for 25 to 30 minutes until cooked – the brownies should still be soft in the middle.
6 Transfer to a wire rack to cool and then cut into pieces.

Extract 5: Hong Kong travel tips

Looking for a tour? Contact us by visiting www.tourism-asia.net

Travelling in a completely unknown place can become a traumatic experience. However, a few travel tips can greatly help. Here is some travel advice for a tour of Hong Kong.

Climate tips

- Hong Kong has four seasons in a year. So one can enjoy different seasons at different times of the year.
- Winter occurs from mid-December until February. Temperatures can plunge to as low as 6 °C.
- Spring runs from March to mid-May and temperatures range from 18–27 °C. A light jacket or sweater would be useful, particularly for the evenings. The atmosphere heats up and humidity soars.
- Autumn runs from September to December and it is a lovely time. Humidity and temperature levels come down.

Language tips

- Chinese and English are the official languages in Hong Kong.
- Many people in Hong Kong do speak English well, but there are many who do not. Many restaurants have their menus only in Chinese.
- It is advisable that you ask your hotel to write your destination address in Chinese, as well as in English, as it might come in useful.

Extract 6: Using your TalkPhone

Using your TalkPhone to call friends and colleagues is straightforward. You can either access the name of the person from your address list by clicking on 'Address Book' in the menu or by keying in their number on the 'Welcome' screen using the keypad. You can also access the name of the person if it appears in your 'Recent Calls' menu. If your phone is linked with the address or phonebook on your home computer, then you can link into this to transfer phone numbers to your TalkPhone. Your voicemail menu also allows you to return a call to anyone who has left you a message.

Making and receiving calls

You are only able to make and receive calls if you are within network range. The indicator at the bottom left of your screen indicates whether you are in range of the network and also indicates the strength of the network signal. Remember that a weak signal means that even though you may be able to make a call, reception may not be particularly clear and you may need to move to a more suitable location to have a satisfactory conversation.

Extract 7: Serena Williams

Serena Jameka Williams was born on 26 September 1981 in Saginaw, Michigan in the USA. She is a professional tennis player who has spent much of her career ranked world number one in singles and world number one in doubles with her sister (Venus Williams). She first became world number one on 8 July 2002. Ranked world number one by the Women's Tennis Association (WTA) five times, she became sixth on the all-time greatest champions list on 3 July 2010.

In 2010 she was the champion in the women's singles and runner-up in the doubles competition (with her sister Venus Williams) at the Australian Open, and the reigning singles champion at Wimbledon. She has won more Grand Slam titles in singles, women's doubles and mixed doubles than any other active female player.

Vital statistics

Height: 5' 9" (1.75 m)
Weight: 150 lb (68 kg)
Plays: Right-handed (two-handed backhand)
Pro since: September 1995

The example extracts on pages 1–6 give a range of factual information in a variety of forms. However, the main purpose of all of them is to communicate this information clearly and concisely. Now answer the following questions about them.

Exercise 1: Extracts 1 to 7

1 Do you think the description of the house in Extract 1 gives enough information to someone who might be interested in buying it? What else do you think should be included?

2 In what type of publication do you think you would find the passage about geysers in Iceland?

3 Explain the meaning of 'dormant' and 'fissures' as used in Extract 2.

4 Why did the Great Geysir start erupting again in 2000?

5 If you were waiting for an Icelandic geyser to erupt, how would you know when it was about to start?

6 Can you find a sentence towards the end of Extract 2 that does not just convey straightforward information? Write down the sentence and say why you think the writer included it.

7 How does the way information is presented in Extract 3 differ from the other examples? Does the way it is presented make it easy for you to understand it?

8 If you were shopping on Scotts Road in Singapore and wanted to catch the earliest available shuttle to the Night Safari, at which two stops could you catch it and at what times?

9 The recipe (Extract 4) contains very few words. Do you think it needs any more detail or explanation? Give reasons for your answer.

10 From Extract 5, list the advantages of visiting Hong Kong in the autumn over visiting in either the winter or spring.

11 Why might it 'come in useful' to have a restaurant address in Hong Kong written down in both Chinese and English?

12 The information about using the TalkPhone in Extract 6 says that making a call is 'straightforward'. Explain, using your own words, how you would make a phone call to a friend who had contacted you earlier.

13 In what type of publication would you find the information in Extract 7?

14 From Extract 7, write down five facts that make Serena Williams a great tennis champion.

The extracts that we have looked at so far have all been quite concise (with some of them being presented in note or table form) as they have all focused on key facts. The extract that follows on pages 8 and 9 is a longer piece of informative writing and is written in a more conventional way. Read it carefully and answer the questions that follow. It is taken from a website aimed at young teenagers.

Pompeii

Have you ever heard of the ancient Italian city called Pompeii? Pompeii was a large and thriving city that was destroyed when a volcano named Mount Vesuvius erupted, killing many of the city's inhabitants and leaving behind a perfectly preserved example of ancient life in the Mediterranean.

Pompeii as it looks today

Two cities, not one

Many people who've heard of Pompeii don't realise there were actually two cities that were destroyed by the eruption of Mount Vesuvius: Pompeii and Herculaneum. Both were completely covered by volcanic ash when Vesuvius belched volcanic ash and hot mud on 24 August in the year AD79.

Pompeii – say *pom–PAY*

Both cities were forgotten until they were found again in the 1700s. Over time the cities became completely buried. Excavation – which is the process archaeologists use to dig up buried artefacts – has been underway for several hundred years. At Pompeii, there are still many, many areas yet to be uncovered.

What was Pompeii like before the explosion?

Pompeii was a city of 20 000 residents. In many ways it was very progressive: Pompeii had indoor running water, a thriving marketplace, an amphitheatre for entertainment and a structured government. The homes of the wealthiest citizens reveal beautiful works of art, particularly frescoes (pictures painted on the walls using a specific technique) and a reverence for the local gods and goddesses.

Pompeii also contained public baths, cobblestone streets, sidewalks and many private shops where its residents could purchase almost anything they wanted. Since Pompeii was a port city, located on the blue waters of the Bay of Naples, the people who lived there could take advantage of the many ships that made port in Pompeii. They brought goods from many other, exotic locations, to trade and sell in Pompeii and other Roman cities.

The people themselves were typical of the Roman empire at that time. There were several classes in Roman society, starting with the very wealthy and ending with slaves. The slaves were usually people who had been captured and enslaved following a war. They served the wealthier Romans and were the lowest class of people in Roman society.

The people of Pompeii wore togas but, like all Romans, only in formal public places as they were considered sacred garments.

What happened when the volcano exploded?

Volcanoes are not all alike. Vesuvius is what is known as a composite volcano. Composite volcanoes have two different types of eruptions: the kind you see in the movies where the volcano spits molten lava and the kind where the volcano spews ash and rock. The eruption that destroyed Pompeii and Herculaneum was of the latter kind.

An ash and rock volcanic eruption like the one that destroyed Pompeii

Many times before an explosion, a volcano will 'rumble' a bit – that is, make noises without actually exploding. Prior to the actual eruption, witnesses reported seeing a very large 'cloud' over the top of the mountain. This cloud was made from volcanic ash and cinders.

The ash from a burned object is usually very light. It looks harmless. But volcanic ash chokes and suffocates every living thing, which is what happened when Vesuvius erupted in AD79. Volcanic ash is thick and heavy and falls in massive amounts, along with hot cinders and rocks. This first stage of eruption is called the 'Plinian stage' of a volcanic eruption.

Pompeii was buried under 8 to 10 feet of ash and debris. Pliny the Younger, a Roman soldier, witnessed much of the eruption and helped to evacuate a small number of residents. The Plinian stage is named for him.

Other disasters also struck Pompeii

Pompeii had its share of natural disasters. In AD62, just 17 years earlier, the city was destroyed by an earthquake, then rebuilt. In the year AD202, Vesuvius erupted for a solid week. In the stretch of time from AD306 to AD522, the volcano erupted at least four times, and maybe as many as five. Vesuvius also erupted in 1631, then again several times in the period from 1913 to 1944. Italians refer to the mountain as 'Vesuvio'.

Excavation of Pompeii

Since its discovery in the 1700s, Pompeii has been in a state of excavation. Many teams of archaeologists have worked on the site, with the result that Pompeii has yielded many artefacts from ancient times. In addition to wonderful frescoes and other objects of art, the town has given us a true picture of life during the Roman era.

Many of the artefacts found in Pompeii are in museums, notably the one in Naples. Sadly, about 2000 bodies were discovered, their outlines preserved forever by the hardened ash, mud and debris.

1)-Pompeii is in Italy

Exercise 2: Pompeii

1 Make notes, using bullet points, of all the factual details about Pompeii and the people who lived there before the eruption of Mount Vesuvius in AD79.

2 Now write a second group of notes containing all the facts about the eruption of Mount Vesuvius and its effects on the surrounding area.

3 Compare the notes you have written for questions 1 and 2 with the original article. What features of the original article have not been included in your note versions of the events. Do you think that these 'missing' features help to make the communication of the facts more interesting to a reader? Give reasons for your answer.

Reading for pleasure

The following two passages are humorous attempts at informative writing. The first sets out to explain the complicated laws of cricket to someone who has no knowledge of the game but in the end only makes them (deliberately!) even more confusing. The second passage is from a website article containing not entirely serious information to younger sisters as to how to get the better of annoying older brothers.

The rules of cricket as explained to a foreign visitor

You have two sides, one out in the field and one in.

Each man that's in the side that's in goes out, and when he's out he comes in and the next man goes in until he's out.

When they are all out, the side that's out comes in and the side that's been in goes out and tries to get those coming in, out. Sometimes you get men still in and not out.

When a man goes out to go in, the men who are out try to get him out, and when he is out he goes in and the next man in goes out and goes in.

There are two men called umpires who stay out all the time and they decide when the men who are in are out.

When both sides have been in and all the men have been out, and both sides have been out twice after all the men have been in, including those who are not out, that is the end of the game!

Advice: How to annoy an older brother

To properly annoy an older brother requires more than just stealing his toys, or pinching him when he's not looking. Psychological annoyance is the way to go. Here are a few ideas (though this list is obviously not exhaustive).

Difficulty: Moderate

Instructions

1 Get him in trouble. Create a situation where your brother will get in trouble. Hit him, and when he hits you back, start crying. This should bring your mother running and earn him a considerable time out, when in fact you are the one who struck first. If he was supposed to do chores, wait until he does them. When he is not looking, undo them (put the garbage back in the kitchen, for example). Write a love note and put it where his girlfriend is sure to find it.

2 Listen in on his phone conversations. Later, use the knowledge to make him very uncomfortable around others – if you heard he has plans to sneak out for a party Friday night, casually suggest a family event that evening. Or better still, suggest an activity where the party is being held ('Wouldn't it be fun to go to that old field and watch the fireflies,' knowing he has a bonfire party in the field that night).

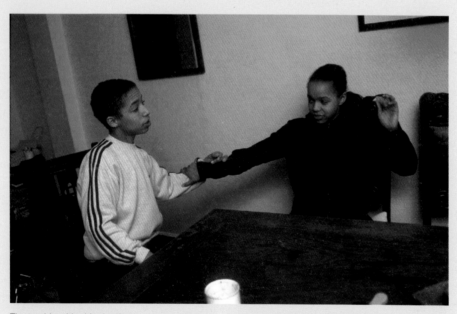

The trouble with older brothers

3 Hide something important of his – homework, sporting equipment, etc. Choose something he needs as a matter of urgency. Wait for him to involve at least four people in his frantic hunt for it. When they have been hunting for about 15 minutes, put the item back somewhere obvious – the chair in his room, his backpack or the kitchen table. He'll be furious and know it was you, but nobody else will.

4 When he brings a new girlfriend home, hang around as much as possible. Suggest that his girlfriend asks him embarrassing questions ('You just have to ask Joe to tell you about the time he split his trousers in school'). Call her the wrong name all night, or refer to stories that involve him and a different girl. Ask her advice on boys/clothes/other girly topics. Make plans to hang out with her, without him.

5 If you're a girl, date one of his friends.

Writing

Activity

Go back to the notes you made about the eruption of Mount Vesuvius (from page 10) and the destruction of Pompeii. Look at the part of the extract that mentions Pliny the Younger, towards the end of the text (page 9). Imagine that you are a friend of Pliny and were with him during the time of the eruption. Describe what you experienced, using the notes you have made, but adding some details from your own imagination.

Extended activity

This is a task which requires you to use both your reading and writing skills. On pages 13–18 is a collection of material about holidaying in the Vendée region of France.

1 Imagine that you and your family spent a holiday in the Vendée last summer in a mobile home on a campsite. This year your uncle, his wife and their three children (aged 7, 10 and 14) who live in the UK are planning to spend their holidays in the same region. They have written to you asking for some detailed factual information about the area. In particular they want to know: about the journey there; what the weather will be like; what type of accommodation they should choose; the campsite and its facilities and what there is in the surrounding area that will be of interest to the whole family. Use the information on pages 13–18 to write your reply.

2 Now, imagine that you are your 14-year-old cousin who is writing to you after the holiday to tell you all about it. This can be a more imaginative, creative piece of writing but you should still base the content of your written account on the material printed on pages 13–18.

Hot air balloon rides in France over Vendée and Deux Sèvres, between Puy du Fou and Marais Poitevin

A flight in a hot air balloon is a unique experience – realise your hot air balloon ride dream during your stay in Vendée. Come along with us and fly over the Vendée countryside.

The hot air balloon flights go in the morning at sunrise and in the evening two hours before sunset.

The entire Skysurfer hot air ballooning experience is approximately four hours long. Flights are approximately one hour in duration. Due to the wind speed and direction, the amount of time aloft in a hot air balloon can never be guaranteed.

Your fun begins immediately when you arrive at our launch fields where you are greeted by Damien and Thomas your pilots and you are briefed about what to expect on your balloon flight.

Flights are daily throughout the year depending on weather conditions.

For take-off times and prices visit our website
http://www.hot-air-balloon-rides.eu/balloon-flight-prices.php

MONTGOLFIERE DU BOCAGE
L'orfosse
79140 CERIZAY
tel 05 49 80 10 45

Why not take your next family holiday in the Vendée,

Take advantage of:
- Easy access from the channel ports (Saint-Malo only three hours to central Vendée).
- The nearest region of France to the UK offering a great climate (on a par with the south).
- Some of the best beaches in France – miles of sand, pine forests and dunes.
- Attractive and varied countryside, sleepy authentic French villages and historic towns.
- Loads to see and do in the Vendée with plenty of activities for the children.

The Vendée is the west coast department of France situated

Come and visit the port at Les Sables d'Olonne.

between Nantes to the north and La Rochelle to the south. It's the second most popular holiday destination in France, welcoming tourists both for family beach holidays and for authentic countryside breaks. It offers excellent value for money being the perfect compromise for distance, weather, accommodation, authentic French life and beautiful scenery.

Travelling to the Vendée

From the western cross channel ferry ports you can easily drive to the Vendée in a day without an overnight stop, making it easily accessible for families with children. From Calais, count on it taking seven to eight hours – still feasible in a day's drive.

For fly-drive to the Vendée you have the nearest choices of either Nantes airport or La Rochelle airport and Poitiers as a possibility further afield. The budget airline companies have regular flights to these airports and car hire is easily available at each, offering a very convenient alternative to the cross channel ferries and often working out very competitive.

west coast of France?

Things to do and places to visit in the Vendée

Apart from just relaxing and taking in some real France, the Vendée offers endless holiday activities with plenty to see and do for young and old alike – theme parks for children of all ages, historic chateaux, towns and villages to visit, son-et-lumière spectacles (sound and light shows), sporting activities, water sports, microlights, go-karts , horse riding, golf …

The Vendée is the second most popular department in France for holidays which is hardly surprising, given its remarkable sunshine record and its magnificent coastline. The Vendée coast attracts many visitors just for the miles of wide sandy beaches, backing onto dunes and pine forests, but also for the typical French fishing ports, the lively resort towns and the remarkably preserved natural sites and nature reserves. It's also well known in the sailing world for the Vendée Globe and prized by many surfing enthusiasts.

But that's not all. Further inland the Vendée countryside has a charm all of its own, from the spectacular open spaces of the reclaimed lands in the south to the unique fens of the Marais Poitevin (Green Venice) and the delicately rolling hills and pastures of the north Vendée Bocage. History and tradition abounds, with a sumptuous rural heritage of chateaux, charming villages, stunning churches and historic towns. Visitors to the Vendée also appreciate the calm of the area – it's so easy to find quiet spots even in high season.

Practical things (shops, opening hours)

As with the rest of France, in the Vendée you will find that many shops close between noon and 2p.m. Bakeries tend to be closed from 1p.m. until late afternoon. The exception to this is the coastal resorts where most shops open all day until late evening. The larger supermarkets are generally open all day, closing around 7.30/8p.m., but please note that most will be closed on Sunday. Plastic carrier bags have now disappeared from most supermarkets, but they sell large reusable bags. For food shopping on Sundays you need to look for the smaller village mini-markets (*superette* in French) which may be open on Sunday mornings.

Other than snack bars and some restaurants in the tourist hot spots, restaurants tend to be strict with their timings, so for lunch you can be served between noon and 1.30p.m. and for evening dinner between 7p.m. and 9.30p.m.

Campsite Les Genêts St Jean Plage

Close to a lovely sandy beach, a lively campsite with both an indoor pool and superb waterpark. Surrounded by attractive woodland, the excellent facilities make Les Genêts ideal for a family holiday. Older children will particularly enjoy a holiday at this lively site. The focal point is the outstanding waterpark with jacuzzi, waterslides, water chute and lazy-river attraction as well as spacious sun terraces and a new modern bar recently added. A short stroll takes you to a beautiful sandy beach or you can explore the woods and dunes along the coast. This site is three quarters of a mile from Merlin Plage, and four miles from St Jean de Monts.

Setting: Beach
Star Rating 4

Opening dates

15/05/2010 – 04/09/2010
Mobiles open: 15/05/2010 – 04/09/2010

Pitches

Number of pitches: 392
Shade: Some have some
Surface: Dust
Tent privacy: Some of the pitches are separated
Mobiles privacy: Some of the pitches are separated

Important information

Vehicles
Are vehicles allowed on pitches: Yes
Extra vehicle charge: €3.00

Out and about
The colourful fishing port of St Gilles Croix de Vie, with its large expanse of golden sand at the Grand Plage, is ten minutes away by car. Further south, Les Sables d'Olonne has a variety of stylish shops and restaurants. Take a boat trip to the traffic-free island of Ile d'Yeu, an island of granite cliffs and rocky creeks and the beautiful rocky Côte Sauvage. Its capital is a lively fishing port where you can sample fresh lobster.

On site

The following facilities are available:

Reception
Languages spoken: English and French
Other services: Fax, post, currency exchange, laundry token, WiFi available
Credit cards accepted: Visa, Mastercard and Eurocard

Shops
Mini-market: Open 17/05/2010 – 07/09/2010
Main shop: Open 17/05/2010 – 07/09/2010

Dining
Restaurant: Small restaurant
Location: Near the pool and bar. Open 17/05/2010 – 07/09/2010
Take-away: Pizzas, burgers, chips, omelettes, daily specials.
Open 17/05/2010 – 07/09/2010

Bars
Bar – modern with terrace, overlooking the pool. Open 17/05/2010

Discos
Family disco: Open 13/06/2010 – 29/08/2010
Children's disco: Open 30/06/2010 – 30/08/2010

Laundry
Washers: 5 x machines €5.00 per load
Dryers: 2 x machines €4.00 per load

Sanitation
Hot showers
Baby baths
Toilets
Children's toilets

Activities

The following activities are available:

Site run children's activities
Games, painting, drawing, face painting
Languages spoken: All
Open 29/06/2010 – 29/08/2010

Watersports
Diving lessons. Open 30/06/2010 – 30/08/2010
Lesson charge: €15.00

Sports
Tennis – one full size court, concrete.
Open 29/04/2010 – 08/09/2010
Charge: €6.00/hour
Equipment hire available: Yes

Table tennis – three tables
Equipment hire available: Yes

Football – one five-a-side pitch, concrete

Badminton – one court

Basketball – one court, concrete. Open 06/05/2010 – 16/09/2010

Volleyball – one court. Open 15/05/2010 – 04/09/2010
Equipment hire available: Yes

Playgrounds
One playground

Cycle hire
Open 17/05/2010 – 07/09/2010
Adults: €41.00/week, €10.00/day
Children: €31.00/week, €10.00/day
Helmets and child seats available

Local attractions

The following local attractions are available:

Nearest beach: La Plage des Marines, 800 m
Nearest river: 10 km
Nearest lake: 20 km

Shopping
Nearest town/village: St Jean de Monts: 5 km

Attractions
Sealand Aquarium de Noirmoutier
A good aquarium with an excellent selection of fish from around the world including warm and cold water fish plus a number of tropical aquariums.

Le Grand Parc Puy du Fou
A reconstruction of an eighteenth century village with villagers in costume. The ruins of a thirteenth century chateau where you can watch a fabulous falconry display or see the Vikings at war. You

can spend hours wandering the grounds and gardens. The evening show is an incredible open-air night show with 850 people and 50 horsemen.

Zoo des Sables d'Olonne
Only a short distance from the enormous Atlantic beaches, the zoo at Les Sables d'Olonne is home to hundreds of animals living in a luxurious setting. Animals include penguins, monkeys, otters, lions, tigers and pandas.

Futuroscope
Theme park for media and technology. Translation headsets are available.

Oceanile
This waterpark in the heart of Noirmoutier is over 37 000 m² and has more than 20 aquatic amusements. With slides and waves there is plenty to ensure that the whole family is entertained.

Speaking and listening

Activity

Think of a place you know well – it could be the town or village in which you live or somewhere that you have visited. Give a talk to your class explaining why it is or is not a good place in which to spend a family holiday.

Key skills

In order to write English confidently and accurately, it is important that you have a sound understanding of the basic mechanics of writing, such as the names and functions of the different parts of speech, punctuation, spelling and grammar and usage. These will be explained at different stages throughout this and later textbooks in the series. We will start with some of the most important points.

Parts of speech

The different words in a sentence have different functions. It is important to know the names of these different parts of speech and to understand how each is used.

Nouns

Nouns are *naming* words – they are the names given to people, places or things. The different types of nouns are listed below:
- **Common noun** is the name given to any unspecified person, place or thing; for example, *boy, city, building*.

Common nouns	Proper nouns	Abstract nouns	Collective nouns
Boy	Taj Mahal	Imagination	Class

- **Proper noun** is the name given to a particular person, place or thing; for example, *Thomas, Buenos Aires, Taj Mahal*.
- **Abstract noun** is the name given to something which does not physically exist, like an idea or a feeling; for example, *imagination, sadness, joy*.
- **Collective noun** is the name given to a single word which is used to represent a collection of people or things; for example, *team, class, congregation*. There is no absolute rule as to whether collective nouns should be considered grammatically as singular or plural. As a general rule, if the collection of things is functioning as a single unit then it is considered as singular; if, however, the noun describes a collection of individuals functioning independently, then it could be seen as plural. It might help to think of the difference between these two statements: *The class was listening closely to the teacher* and *The class were chatting and drawing in their notebooks*.

Exercise: Identifying nouns

Make a list of the nouns in the following paragraph and write the type of noun next to each one.

My grandfather was a man of great energy and enthusiasms. When he was younger he played football for a local club and was captain of the team. Their matches were played on a pitch at Greentrees, which was the name of a public park near where my grandfather lived. Every Saturday afternoon he was watched by an audience of small children and their parents who were amazed at the skills that he and his teammates displayed.

— Grandfather, man, enthusiasms ; he ; football ; club ; team ;
— Greentrees ; park ; parents ; teammates ; children.

Verbs

Verbs are words which describe an action or a state of being and are central to the structure of a sentence. For example:

1 The boy *broke* the window.
2 The dog *barked*.
3 The ugly duckling *became* a swan.

In each of these examples the verb is the word written in italics. The noun that performs the action of the verb (*boy*, *dog*, *duckling*) is referred to as the **subject** of the verb.

In the first example, the verb *broke* is followed by the noun *window*. In a sentence like this, the noun that follows the verb is known as the **object** of the verb and is said to 'suffer' the action of the verb. A verb which is followed by an object is called a **transitive** verb.

In the second example, there is no object in the sentence. In this case, the verb *barked* – which is not followed by an object – is called an **intransitive** verb. (Some verbs can be either transitive or intransitive depending on how they are used.)

Finally, verbs can describe a state of being as well as an action – like *became* in the third example. The subject of the verb in this example (*the ugly duckling*) and the word that follows the verb (*swan*) refer to the same thing – words following verbs like *become* are known as **complements** because they *complete* the sense of the sentence.

A **finite** or **main** verb is a form of a verb which describes an action or state of being which is complete in itself. It has tense (past, present or future) and number (singular or plural), for example:

I *played* tennis.
She *eats* her breakfast.
It *will be* a fine day tomorrow.

All of these simple sentences make sense and it is because of the verbs in each one.

Another feature of a finite verb is that it can be either **active** or **passive**. In the active, the subject of the verb performs the action ('The boy *kicked* the football') whereas if the verb is in the passive, the subject suffers the action of the verb ('The football *was kicked* by the boy').

Exercise: Identifying verbs

List the verbs in the following sentences. Then copy and complete the table that follows.

1 Steven ate his lunch quickly.
2 He was very keen to play football.
3 The spectators cheered as Steven scored a goal.
4 The sweet shop owner spoke kindly to Helen.

5 Helen's mother asked a difficult question.
6 The football smashed the sweet shop window.
7 The boys were sorry for breaking the window but the sweet shop owner told them they would have to pay for the damage.

Verb	Transitive/ Intransitive	Subject of verb	Object of verb (if there is one)	Complement (if there is one)

Sentence types and structures

Once you understand the ways verbs work, you will also see how important they are in making sentences complete and make sense. It is especially important to understand how the presence or absence of a main verb in your writing affects how clearly your meaning is communicated to your reader.

Some definitions

A **phrase** is a group of words which does not contain a finite or main verb; for example, 'The lion, *lying quietly in the bushes*, seemed completely harmless.' The words in italics are a phrase which, in this case, describes the lion. However, they would not make complete sense if used on their own – the verb *seemed* and its complement are necessary for the full meaning to be communicated.

A **clause** is a group of words which does contain a finite verb. There are two types of clauses: **main clauses** and **subordinate clauses**. A main clause is a single unit which can stand on its own and make complete sense; for example, 'Juan hurried to school.' However, a subordinate clause does not make complete sense on its own and needs the main clause to which it relates to be understood; for example, 'Juan hurried to school *because he had overslept and missed his bus*.' (the subordinate clause is in italics). In this sentence, although the subordinate clause provides further information about why Juan was hurrying it does not make sense to a reader without the main clause which comes before it.

A sentence, therefore, must contain at least one main clause. A sentence that contains just one main clause is known as a **simple sentence**. A sentence containing two or more main clauses joined by a **conjunction** such as 'and' ('Juan overslept and then he missed his bus to school.') is known as a **compound sentence**. Finally, a sentence which contains a mixture of main and subordinate clauses ('Juan missed the bus, which he had hoped to catch to school, and then had to run all the way to get there before the bell rang.') is known as a **complex sentence**. Usually, complex sentences need conjunctions to link the different clauses together.

Forming complex sentences

Read and consider the following sentences.

1 *Amber was late for school because she had forgotten to set her alarm clock.*

In this sentence, the main clause is *Amber was late for school* and the subordinate clause is *she had forgotten to set her alarm clock* (the subordinate clause does not make sense on its own as it is **dependent** on the main clause). The word *because* is a conjunction that joins the two clauses together.

2 *The chest, which contained all the pirates' gold, was buried beneath the tallest tree on the island.*

In this sentence, the main clause is *The chest … was buried beneath the tallest tree on the island* and the subordinate clause is *which contained all the pirates' gold*. This is joined to the main clause by the relative pronoun *which*.

Remember: clauses are joined by **conjunctions** and **relative pronouns** (such as *who, that, which*) – they are *not* joined by putting a comma between them. This is not one of the functions of a comma!

In your own writing, you should try to vary the types of sentences you use in order to give variety to your expression – too many simple sentences soon become monotonous. As a general rule, the more complicated your ideas are, the more you are likely to use lengthy sentences. However, short sentences can be very effective as a way to make or emphasise a point. Good writers will make sure that their writing contains a mixture of sentence types that are appropriate to the tone and purpose of their writing.

Exercise: Identifying phrases and clauses

Identify whether the words in italics below are phrases or clauses and explain the purpose of each of them (e.g. [the phrase/clause] acts as an adjective/noun, etc.).

I was fascinated by the strange house *with the green door, standing in the middle of the forest*. Every afternoon, *after I had finished school*, I walked past there, *lost in thought*, wondering if its inhabitants were real or ghosts. One day, the gate *that led into their garden* was standing *wide open*. I plucked up courage and walked bravely *up to the front door*. It was locked but, *from deep inside the house*, I could hear singing and laughter.

Exercise: Joining sentences

In each of the five examples that follow, combine the pairs or groups of short sentences into one longer sentence. You can leave out words and alter the wording where necessary. Try not to rely too much on using simple conjunctions such as *and*.

1 One morning I went for a walk. It had rained hard earlier. There were deep puddles in the roads. The traffic was moving very slowly.

2 My school is to be found in the busiest part of the town. It is a brand new building with a lot of windows. It is a very attractive building.

3 My mother works very hard. She gets up very early in the morning. She makes breakfast for all the family. She goes to work when she has done this.

4 We had been walking for the whole day. It seemed as if our hike was never going to end. The forest became thicker and thicker. At last we saw the campsite in a clearing ahead of us.

5 Maria left home very early in the morning. She drove her car as quickly as she could. She had a very long way to travel. Her best friend's wedding was taking place that afternoon.

Punctuation

Full stops

A sentence is a group of words which begins with a capital letter and ends with a full stop, exclamation or question mark and contains a main verb. It is, therefore, a complete unit of sense.

A **full stop** (sometimes referred to as a 'period') is used to mark the end of a sentence; for example, 'It was the start of the holidays and the sun was shining brightly. For once, Lee did not want to stay in bed and go back to sleep.' Here there are two separate statements each containing a main verb and each with a different subject; it is, therefore, correct to show the pause between them by using a full stop.

Try to think in complete sentences when you are writing so that you become used to using full stops whenever you complete a particular unit of sense. One of the most common causes of confusion for a reader is when the writer has not used full stops correctly.

Exercise: Full stops

Rewrite the following extract from a guide to the English city of Brighton, putting in full stops and capital letters where necessary.

There should be ten full stops in total.

Brighton is on the South Coast of the United Kingdom, about 50 minutes by train from London Brighton has always been a place of fun and nowadays offers an 'in scene', beachfront, history, restaurants, hotels, lively arts scene and lots of local attractions in the Sussex countryside, making it a great place for wonderful holidays along the seafront, there are several traditional fish and chip shops and souvenir stands the Victorian-style Brighton Pier juts out into the English Channel and is full of restaurants and amusement arcades that cater mostly to children and families however, don't expect sandy beaches Brighton's beach consists of pebbles although it may not be the most comfortable place for sunbathing, it is the perfect place for taking an afternoon stroll aside from its many seaside delights,

Brighton is also home to some historic treasures the Royal Pavilion brings a touch of royalty to the seaside once the seaside retreat of the Prince Regent (who later became King George IV), the exterior of this nineteenth century pleasure palace bears a striking resemblance to some of India's most magnificent palaces

Brighton pier

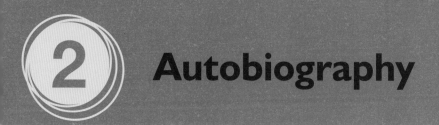

Autobiography

Reading

All of us will have special memories of things that we experienced when we were younger. They may have been personal to us or they may be things which we shared with friends or families. Here are two memories of growing up in the city of Liverpool in England.

The first was written by the England soccer captain, Steven Gerrard, and in it he tells us about how he behaved when he was at primary school in the 1980s (note that Merseyside is the name given for the area around the city of Liverpool, Ironside is the name of the area where Steven Gerrard lived in the city and Bluebell is a nearby park).

Steven Gerrard

The second is by Helen Forrester who grew up in a poor area of the same city nearly 60 years earlier. In the extract she describes her attempt to get a job in a sweet shop, with the 'help' of her mother who, despite having no money, believed that her daughter was better than her financial position suggested. Read both passages carefully and answer the questions that follow.

Extract 1: *Gerrard – My Autobiography*

Still now I hate Sunday nights. Still! It's impossible to blank out the memory of getting ready for school, a ritual torture that ruined the final moments of a glorious weekend. According to the calendar most people use, a weekend lasts two days. Not at No. 10 Ironside. Not with Mum. A weekend is a day and a half with her. She demanded we be home by 6p.m. to be scrubbed, bathed and ready for school the next morning. We ran in at six and the uniform was there, on the ironing board, all pristine and pressed glaring at us. Just seeing the uniform made me sick. They resembled prison clothes after the freedom of the weekend. It was not that I hated school; I just loved my weekends roaming around Bluebell. Mum took school more seriously than Paul, my brother, and I ever did. A proud woman, she made sure our uniforms were absolutely spotless. She polished our shoes so hard you could see your grimacing face in them. Poor Mum! She had her work cut out. If I left the house with a clean uniform, it was guaranteed to come home dirty. The same with shoes. Scuffed and muddy. Every time. Mum went up the wall.

[handwritten:] ecause still now hate sunday nights. Sitll ! It's impossible to blank out the memory getting ready for school, a ritual torture that ruined the final moment of a glorious we

25

My journey through the Merseyside school system was straightforward and undistinguished. I looked on schools as fantastic playing fields with boring buildings attached. My first stop was St Michael's, which became Huyton-with-Roby Church of England Primary. Though only a short walk from Ironside, Mum still insisted on driving me to St Mick's and picking me up. I enjoyed the infants and junior school, just messing about. When I was naughty, the teachers made me stand by the wall, looking at the bricks for five minutes as punishment. I never bullied anyone. I never hurt anyone or swore. I was just cheeky and mischievous. My crimes were petty ones: answering back or going on muddy grass when we were told to stay on the yard. Usual kids' stuff.

School held limited appeal. I sat in class, longing for playtime because there was always a match on in the playground. I loved dinner time because it lasted an hour, which meant a longer match. I abandoned hot dinners because they wasted precious minutes. Queuing for my meal, I'd shout, 'Come on, there's a big game going on out there.' Eventually, I asked my mother for packed lunches. 'You should be on hot dinners,' she screamed, 'or come home if you don't like school food.' We compromised on packed lunches: sandwich, bar of chocolate and drink. And some fruit. The fruit always came home untouched. Apples, bananas and oranges weren't me. Butties [sandwiches] weren't even me at that age. It would be bread off, meat out, quick bite, on with the game. 'Stevie, you haven't eaten your butty,' Mum would say, 'you've only eaten your chocolate.' Mum didn't understand. Speed was vital at dinner time. I ate the packed lunch while playing or wolfed it down running back into class. Same with my tea. If there was a match going on outside Ironside, a game of chase, or my mates were waiting for me, I slipped my food in my pocket, sprinted out the door, threw the food to the neighbour's dog and raced on to the match. I returned home starving, picking at biscuits, crisps and chocolate.

Back at St Mick's, the teachers watched me scribbling away busily in my school book. Steam almost rose from my pencil I wrote so furiously. The teachers must have thought I was focusing really hard on the lesson. I'm sorry. I wasn't. Lessons were spent working out the teams for dinner time. In the back of my school book, I wrote down the names. When the bell for break rang, I dashed out to organise all the boys – and get the girls off the playground. 'You can watch,' I'd tell them generously, 'but that's the pitch and you can't go on it.' The pitch was marked out with bags and tops for goals. They were right serious battles at St Mick's. Wembley Cup finals have been less intense. My face still bears the trace of a scar collected in the playground after I collided with a fence, tussling for the ball. Defeat was unthinkable.

Steven Gerrard

because the doesn't want to came home early

Answer these questions about Extract 1. You can either write down your responses or talk through them with your teacher or a partner.

Exercise 1: Steven Gerrard

1 Why did Steven Gerrard hate Sunday nights?

2 Why does he say that to his mother a weekend was only a day and a half?

3 What is meant by 'Mum went up the wall' and what did Steven do to make it happen?

4 Give the meaning of each of the following words as it is used in the passage:

grimacing
guaranteed
undistinguished
petty
compromised

5 Explain using your own words how Steven looked on the schools he attended.

6 Choose three details from the passage that show that Steven was fanatical about football and explain how the examples you have chosen show this.

7 Imagine that you are the Headteacher at Steven's primary school. Using what you have learnt about him from this passage, write his school report. You should write two or three paragraphs.

Extract 2: *Liverpool Miss*

It was a very little shop, in a shabby block of other small shops and offices. Its window, however, sparkled with polishing despite the overcast day. Through the gleaming glass I could dimly see rows of large bottles of sweets and in front of them an arrangement of chocolate boxes, all of them free of dust. Beneath the window, a sign in faded gold lettering advertised Fry's Chocolate.

Mother, who had not spoken to me during the walk, paused in front of the shop and frowned. Then she swung open the glass-paned door and stalked in. I followed her, my heart going pit-a-pat, in unison with the click of Mother's shoes on the highly polished, though worn, linoleum within.

An old-fashioned bell hung on a spring attached to the door was still tinkling softly when a stout, middle-aged woman with a beaming smile on her round face emerged through a lace-draped door leading to an inner room.

'Yes, luv?' she inquired cheerfully.

'I understand that you wrote to my daughter about a post in your shop?' Mother's voice was perfectly civil, but the word 'post' instead of 'job' sounded sarcastic.

The smile was swept from the woman's face. She looked us both up and down uncertainly, while I agonised over what Mother might say next.

'Helen?' the woman asked, running a stubby finger along her lower lip.

'Helen Forrester,' replied Mother icily.

'Ah did.' The voice had all the inflections of a born Liverpudlian. She looked past Mother, at me standing forlornly behind her. Her thoughtful expression cleared, and she smiled slightly at me. I smiled shyly back.

I felt her kindness like an aura round her and sensed that I would enjoy being with her, even if she did expect a lot of work from me.

'Have you ever worked before, luv?' she asked me, running fingers on which a wedding ring gleamed through hair which was improbably golden.

I nodded negatively. Then cleared my throat and said, 'Only at home.'

'What work would Helen be expected to do?' asked Mother, her clear voice cutting between the woman and me like a yacht in a fast wind. She had also the grace of a yacht in the wind; but the sweet shop owner was obviously finding her more trying than graceful and answered uncertainly, 'Well, now, I hadn't exactly thought. I need a bit o' help, that's all. 'Course she'd have to wash the floor and polish it, like, every day. And clean the window and dust the stock. And when I knowed her a bit she could probably help me with serving, like. I get proper busy at weekends – and in summer the ice cream trade brings in a lot o' kids, and you have to have eyes in the back o' your head or they'll steal the pants off you.'

Mother sniffed at this unseemly mention of underwear, and then nodded.

'And what would the salary be?' I groaned inwardly. I was sure that in a little shop like this one earned wages not a salary.

The beginning of a smile twitched at the woman's lips, but she answered Mother gravely.

'Well, I'd start her on five shillings, and if she was any good I'd raise it.'

Even in those days, five shillings was not much. The woman seemed to realise this, because she added, 'And o' course, she can eat as many sweets as she likes. But no taking any out of the shop.'

I could imagine that this was not as generous as it sounded. After a week of eating too many sweets, the desire for them would be killed and few people would want them any more.

Helen Forrester

Answer these questions about Extract 2.

Exercise 2: Helen Forrester

1 Give the meaning of each of the following words or phrases as it is used in the passage:

in unison
inflections
forlornly
an aura
hair which was improbably golden

2 What made the sweet shop stand out among the other shops in the area?

3 Explain in your own words why Helen thought her mother sounded sarcastic when she asked about the 'post' that was available.

4 Give three differences between Mother and the sweet shop owner and explain how these details help you to understand the characters of the two women.

5 Imagine you are the sweet shop owner. Using information you have gathered from the passage, write two paragraphs giving your thoughts about Helen and her mother.

In both of these descriptions, the writers are describing their lives as children; for example, Steven Gerrard tells us a lot about his thoughts about going to school and, in particular, how football completely dominated his life.

Helen Forrester, rather than telling us in great detail what her feelings were, gives us her memory of a particular episode in her childhood. Through this she allows us to understand and share her thoughts and to gain an understanding of her mother's character and their relationship. We also learn something about what it was like growing up in an industrial city during the economic depression of the 1930s.

Both passages also include details which help to bring alive the situations they describe – for example, Steven's description of the school lunch hour and the details that Helen gives us about her mother and the shopkeeper.

The two passages are both from early on in the writers' accounts and so it is important that they include some factual information. The following extract, however, adopts a slightly different approach. The writer, Amryl Johnson, now an adult, is revisiting the Caribbean island of Tobago where she grew up as a child. In this passage she describes a somewhat eccentric activity that she witnessed during her visit. In her account she attempts not just to describe what took place, but also, through her use of language, to recreate the atmosphere surrounding the event.

Extract 3: The goat race

I was about to witness goat racing. A little later, there would be crab racing. Easter Monday in Buccoo Village. I was fighting my way through ice-cream vans, hordes of people, food stalls and hot music singeing my eardrums. Even though the general movement was towards the racecourse, I elbowed my way through the crowds in an effort to get a good pitch. An area had been cordoned off to make a course for competitors. Not quite on a par with the traditional racing scale but on a parallel assumption that spectators were to line either side of a stretch of ground along which the participants would travel.

I had been walking around the site, soaking in the atmosphere and enjoying being on my own. My friends would find me from time to time to phrase a variation of the same question.

'You want anything? You want ice-cream, sweet bread, roti, a plate of stewed beef and rice, souse, black pudding, sugar cake?'

I told them yes to the first question and no to the rest. I had had more than my fair share of breakfast that morning. Salt fish cooked with tomatoes and onions, washed down with a big cup of real chocolate was a heavier breakfast than I was used to. However, I was quickly getting accustomed to the change.

Some people take this event very seriously. I have been told that money changes hands. 'The goats are looking frisky.' I wish I could have used that expression to describe what I saw. The glazed preoccupation of the goats as they stood chewing their cuds made them look anything but 'frisky'. You will not find jockeys seated on their mounts here. Good job too! Feel sure they would have the Tobagonian equivalent of the RSPCA [Royal Society for the Prevention of Cruelty to Animals] down on them like a ton of bricks. An attempt was being made to keep a handful of select goats in order. No mean achievement when dealing with an animal fabled to eat almost anything it can lay its mouth to. Around each animal's neck was a rope. At the end of each rope was a man holding a stick. Part of the uniform looked authentic. The trousers were white, near white, off white, and looked the sort of clothes you would expect to be worn by anyone taking part in an exercise of that nature. In that respect one could call the men minders. Bare feet, teeshirt or vest, identification number completed the ensemble.

And they were off! I soon got the idea. It was how quickly you and your quadruped could race the other men and theirs to the finishing line. Bare feet and hooves pounded stones further into the ground. The humans were moving as if their lives depended on it. The goats were probably certain their lives did. Curried goat is a delicacy on the islands. First one across the line got cooked? Or was it the last one to cross who went into the pot? Either way, it would be best to play safe and stay close to the middle. The tension on the rope was nail-biting. There is always one. There is always one soul who remains oblivious to ruin. The hooves of one billy were thudding on the quaking earth as if his life would begin when he reached the finishing line. His minder looked a worried man. He had reason. His feet had hardly touched the ground since the race began. He was hanging on to the end of the rope with both hands — must be some sort of life raft — and being tugged to the finishing line. He was declared the winner. Rumour had it the goat ended up in the pot, anyway. They had to throttle it to get it to stop running. The minder responded to everyone who congratulated him with the same surprised, bewildered smile.

Amryl Johnson

Answer these questions about Extract 3.

Exercise 3: Amryl Johnson

1 Explain the meaning of the word 'singeing' as used by the writer in the first paragraph. Why do you think she uses this word to suggest the effect of the music?

2 What is the writer suggesting by saying 'However, I was quickly getting accustomed to the change' at the end of paragraph 4?

3 Why do you think that 'money changes hands' at the goat racing track?

4 Describe using your own words the 'ensemble' worn by the minders of the goats. What do you think the writer's opinion is of these 'minders'?

5 Explain fully why you think that the minder of the winning goat was left with a 'surprised, bewildered smile'.

6 By referring closely to the whole passage, say what you think the writer's attitude was to her goat racing experience.

In this passage, the writer is recreating a colourful and exotic experience by using imaginative language to convey the precise details of a particular episode. Although the surroundings in which the event took place were those with which she was familiar as a child, she is also seeing them as someone who is now a visitor to the area rather than a native of the place. As a result, her feelings are a mixture of amusement and familiarity which helps to put the event into perspective.

With a partner, read through the passage again and make notes on the ways in which the writer describes details in her attempt to recreate the liveliness of the occasion. Copy and complete the following table which may help you to record your notes. The first example has been done for you.

Specific detail	How it works
I was fighting my way through ice-cream vans, hordes of people, food stalls and hot music singeing my eardrums.	*This sentence brings alive the many sensations felt by the writer as she makes her way to the track. She is surrounded by 'hordes' of excitable people but the ice-cream vans and food stalls remind us that this is a good-natured public holiday event and the 'hot music' burning into her ears shows how much she is becoming part of the whole experience.*

Reading for pleasure

Here are two poems about childhood and school.

'I Am the Child'

I am the child,
All the world waits for my coming
All the earth watches with interest
To see what I shall become.
The future hangs in the balance,
For what I am
The world of tomorrow will be.

I am the child,
I have come into your world
about which I know nothing.
Why I came I know not.
How I came I know not.
I am curious
I am interested.

I am the child,
You hold in your hand my destiny.
You determine, largely,
whether I shall succeed or fail.
Give me, I pray you,
Those things that make for happiness.
Train me, I beg you,
That I may be a blessing to the world.

Mamie Gene Cole

*This poem, written in Chinese and English, appears at the
entrance to the Guideposts Kindergarten in Hong Kong.*

'Your School'

Your school knows the names of places –
Dhaka, Rajshahi, Sylket, Khulna, Chittagong
and where they are.
Your school knows where rivers rise –
the Ganges, Brahmaputra, Thames –
and knows which seas they join.

Your school knows the height of mountains
disappearing into cloud.
Your school knows important dates,
the days when history turned around
to stare the human race
straight in the face.

Your school knows the poets' names, long dead –
John Keats, Rabindranath Tagore, Sylvia Plath –
and what they said.
It knows the paintings hanging in the old gold frames
in huge museums
and how the artists lived and loved
who dipped their brushes in the vivid paint.

Your school knows the language of the world –
hello, namaskar, sat sri akal, as-salaam-o-aleykum, salut –
it knows the homes of faith,
the certainties of science,
the living art of sport.

Your school knows what Isaac Newton thought,
what William Shakespeare wrote
and what Mohammed taught.

Your school knows your name –
Shirin, Abdul, Aysha, Rayhan, Lauren, Jack –
and who you are.
Your school knows the most important thing to know
you are a star,
a star.

Carol Ann Duffy

Writing

Now that you've looked at examples of autobiographical writing it's time to attempt a piece of your own.

Activity

Write an article entitled 'When I Was Younger' for a magazine aimed at people of your age group. You should write about one or two memorable experiences that you had when you were of primary school age. You could choose to write about things that happened to you in school or when you were with family or friends.

Use the following suggestions to help you plan your writing.

What should I write about?

You've been given a general topic to write about but the decision as to precisely what it will be is yours alone. Try to choose to write about some things that you actually experienced – so you could choose to describe your first morning at a new school, a family celebration or an outing that you enjoyed. What you write should be based on fact although there's nothing wrong with embellishing some details to make things more interesting for your reader!

How much should I write?

Remember, this is an article for a magazine so it shouldn't be too long. You should aim to write about five or six reasonably sized paragraphs and focus on communicating clearly what happened. Don't try to include too many details – rather than, for example, trying to describe the whole of a week's holiday, concentrate instead on just one key element of it (the journey to the holiday resort, for example).

Who am I writing this for?

You are writing this for readers of the magazine, who are of your age group. Try to write informally so that you address your readers in a friendly way and express your own personality. Remember though to use standard English so that your teacher can also understand what you are writing!

How should I organise my writing?

It's worth spending a few minutes before you start to write thinking about this question. For example, are you going to describe the event exactly as it happened? That is, by starting with what happened first and then going through the details in a logical and straightforward way or do you want to start with what the outcome of the experience was and then gradually reveal the events leading up to it? Do you want to focus mainly on describing what actually happened or do you want to spend more time writing about your feelings and the way you responded to what happened? The answer to these (and other thoughts that you might have) are, of course, entirely down to you, but it's important to ask these questions as doing so will help you to produce a piece of writing which is both interesting and consistent in its approach.

What words will best capture the experience?

You've already decided that you will take an informal approach to writing your account but don't be overly chatty in your writing. Make sure that you have a clear picture in your mind of the details of the event and then think about choosing the best words to describe them and to make them come alive in the minds of your readers. Think carefully about the small details which will make the descriptions clearer. Think about the verbs and adverbs that you use: 'The teacher led us into the room' does little more than state a fact whereas 'The teacher strode purposefully into the room and we followed eagerly' gives a much clearer picture of what happened.

Speaking and listening

> Activity
>
> Prepare a talk of about four to five minutes to give to your class or a small group in which you explain how certain toys, pets, books or other possessions that you had when you were younger had a particular influence on you as you were growing up. Prepare some notes to help you during your talk and, if possible, bring in some of the things you talk about to act as visual aids – this may prove difficult if your pet is a particularly lively or scary creature!

Key skills

Parts of speech

In Chapter 1 we learnt about nouns and verbs; in this chapter we will be looking at other main parts of speech.

Pronouns

A pronoun is a word used in place of a noun, for example: *I, you, he, she, it, we, they, this, that, anyone, anybody*. Using pronouns is a way of keeping unnecessary and awkward repetition out of your writing. For example:

> Eric and his sister went to the market to shop. When Eric and his sister arrived there Eric and his sister found that Eric and his sister were too late as all the best things had already been sold.

It would be more effectively expressed using pronouns:

> Eric and his sister went to the market to shop. When *they* arrived there, *they* found that *they* were too late as all the best things had already been sold.

Adjectives

An adjective is a word used to describe a noun, for example:

> The *new* school had *shiny glass* windows which allowed the children *exciting* views of the town.

Adverbs

An adverb is a word which qualifies (that is, adds to the meaning of) a verb, an adjective or another adverb. Many, but not all, adverbs end in –ly. In the first of the following examples an adverb is used to modify the meaning of a verb; in the second the adverb modifies an adjective; and in the third, one adverb modifies another:

> The boy walked to school *slowly*.
> I ate a *very* large dinner.
> It was raining *quite heavily*.

Prepositions

A preposition is a word used with a noun or pronoun to show the connection between persons or things. Common prepositions include:

> about, above, across, against, along, around, at, before, behind, beneath, beside, between, by, down, during, except, for, from, near, off, on, over, round, since, till, towards, under, until, up, upon

Conjunctions and interjections

A conjunction is a word used to connect words or groups of words. For example:

and, or, but, however

An interjection is a word used to express a feeling such as joy or anger and is usually followed by an exclamation mark. For example:

What! Oh! Hurray!

Punctuation

Apostrophes

Apostrophes are used for two main purposes: the first one is quite straightforward; the second is more complicated.

1 To indicate when a letter or letters have been missed out of a word (when a word or words have been contracted). For example: *I didn't understand that. It's not fair. You weren't paying attention.*
2 To indicate possession. In English the possessive form of a noun is shown as follows:
   a) In the singular, the possessive form is made by adding –'s. For example:

bird	the bird's nest
boy	the boy's football
school	the school's classroom

   b) When the plural form of a noun is made by adding –s to the singular, the possessive is shown by adding an apostrophe after the –s (s'). For example:

birds	the birds' nests
boys	the boys' footballs
schools	the schools' classrooms

   c) When the plural form of a noun is *not* made by adding –s, the possessive is shown by adding –'s. For example:

men	the men's cars
children	the children's books
women	the women's changing room

The apostrophe is required in expressions like: a month's wait; a week's holiday; an hour's journey.

Remember: **it's** = *it is* but **its** = *belonging to it.*

Exercise: Apostrophes

Rewrite the following sentences using apostrophes where appropriate.

1 Alawiahs books were lost somewhere in her fathers office.
2 Excuse me, sir, can you tell me whats happened to my dog?
3 Its getting late and its time you were in bed.
4 The teachers desk was piled high with the students exercise books.
5 I went to fetch my mothers shopping that she had left in the ladies gym.
6 'Wheres my book?' said Sanjeev. 'I must have left it at Bhaveshs house.'
7 The boys bedrooms were full of childrens games.
8 'Whos this?' asked the teacher.
9 Anitas face was red when she realised that she had taken Nasrins book by mistake.
10 Im not going to visit the dentists surgery any more; its old and I don't like the rooms smell.

3 Descriptive writing

Reading

When you are writing something imaginative – such as a story or an account of an interesting personal experience – you can make your writing more effective by including detailed descriptions of people and places. To write effective descriptions, you need a clear picture in your mind of who or what it is that you are setting out to describe. Doing this allows you to focus on precise details which make the descriptions come alive in the reader's mind. Good writers incorporate descriptive passages into the overall piece of writing rather than write descriptively for the sake of it.

A good rule to follow in writing descriptions is to base what you describe on your own experiences. This doesn't mean that writers always describe exactly what they have seen or people they have met, but that they use their real life experiences as a *basis* for their descriptions and then develop them from there.

Here are five examples of descriptive writing (Extracts 1 to 5). Read the passages carefully and answer the questions that follow. All of these passages are taken from books written in the last 150 years or so (the earliest was published in 1854). Extracts 1 and 2 describe very hot days in the countryside. Extract 1 is set on the island of Jamaica in the Caribbean; Extract 2 is set in Botswana in Southern Africa.

Extract 1: *A High Wind in Jamaica*

The sun was still red and large: the sky above cloudless, and light blue glaze poured over baking clay: but close over the ground a dirty grey haze hovered. As they followed the lane towards the sea they came to a place where, yesterday, a fair-sized spring had bubbled up by the roadside. Now it was dry. But even as they passed some water splashed out, and then it was dry again, although gurgling inwardly to itself. But the group of children were hot, far too hot to speak to one another: they sat on their ponies as loosely as possible, longing for the sea.

The morning advanced. The heated air grew quite easily hotter, as if from some enormous furnace from which it could draw at will. Bullocks only shifted their stinging feet when they could bear the soil no longer: even the insects were too lethargic to pipe, the basking lizards hid themselves and panted. It was so still you could have heard the least buzz a mile off. Not a naked fish would willingly move his tail. The ponies advanced because they must. The children ceased even to think.

Richard Hughes

Exercise 1: A High Wind in Jamaica

1 From Extract 1 choose three details that convey the extreme heat of the day. Give reasons for your choice.
2 How did the heat affect the children?
3 Explain, using your own words, how the animal life responded to the heat.
4 Later in the day, a hurricane hits the area. How do the descriptions in the passage suggest that something serious is about to happen?

Extract 2: *The No. 1 Ladies' Detective Agency*

Suddenly she saw the house, tucked away behind the trees almost in the shadow of the hill. It was a bare earth house in the traditional style; brown mud walls, a few glassless windows, with a knee-height wall around the yard. A previous owner, a long time ago, had painted designs on the wall, but neglect and the years had scaled them off and only their ghosts remained ... She opened the door and eased herself out of the van. The sun was riding high; its light prickled at her skin. They were too far west here, too close to the Kalahari Desert, and her unease increased. This was not the comforting land she had grown up with; this was the merciless Africa, the waterless land.

Alexander McCall Smith

Exercise 2: The No. 1 Ladies' Detective Agency

1 From Extract 2 choose three words or phrases that suggest that the house and its surroundings were unwelcoming and hostile. Give reasons for your choice.

2 Explain the effects of the sun on the woman in the passage.

3 What was it that she did not like about this part of the Kalahari Desert?

4 We learn in the book that the lady detective is visiting the house of a murderer. How does the description of the house and its surroundings emphasise this point?

Extracts 3 and 4 describe living beings. Gerald Durrell was a naturalist, conservationist and zoo keeper. In Extract 3 he describes a family of young hedgehogs that he looked after when he was a young boy. Charles Dickens, on the other hand, describes an unpleasant nineteenth century factory owner in his novel *Hard Times* in Extract 4.

Extract 3: *Birds, Beasts and Relatives*

They are covered with a thick coating of spikes but these are white and soft, as though made of rubber. They gradually harden and turn brown when the babies are a few weeks old. When they are old enough to leave the nursery the mother leads them out and shows them how to hunt for food; they walk in line, the tail of one held in the mouth of the baby behind. The baby at the head of the column holds tight to mother's tail with grim determination, and they move through the twilit hedgerows like a strange prickly centipede …

Mine were always ready for food at any hour of the day or night. You had only to touch the box and a chorus of shrill screams arose from four little pointed faces poking out of the leaves, each head decorated with a crew-cut of white spikes; and the little black noses would wave desperately from side to side in an effort to locate the bottle.

Most baby animals know when they have had enough, but in my experience this does not apply to baby hedgehogs. Like four survivors from a raft, they flung themselves on to the bottle and sucked and sucked and sucked as though they had not had a decent meal in weeks. If I had allowed it they would have drunk twice as much as was good for them. As it was, I think I tended to overfeed them, for their tiny legs could not support the weight of their fat bodies, and they would advance across

the carpet with a curious swimming motion, their tummies dragging on the ground. However, they progressed very well: their legs grew stronger, their eyes opened, and they would even make daring excursions as much as 15 centimetres away from their box.

Gerald Durrell

Exercise 3: Birds, Beasts and Relatives

1 From Extract 3 write down six facts that you learn about hedgehogs.
2 Choose four words or phrases from the passage that refer to the hedgehogs as if they were human children. How does each of these expressions help you to imagine the appearance and behaviour of the animals?
3 Explain, using your own words, the way in which the hedgehogs drank from the bottle of milk.
4 Explain, using your own words, the effect of having drunk too much milk on the hedgehogs.

Extract 4: *Hard Times*

He was a rich man: banker, merchant, manufacturer, and what not. A big, loud man, with a stare, and a metallic laugh. A man made out of a coarse material, which seemed to have been stretched to make so much of him. A man with a great puffed head and forehead, swelled veins in his temples, and such a strained skin to his face that it seemed to hold his eyes open, and lift his eyebrows up. A man with a pervading appearance on him of being inflated like a balloon, and ready to start. A man who could never sufficiently vaunt himself a self-made man. A man who was always proclaiming, through that brassy speaking-trumpet of a voice of his, his old ignorance and his old poverty. A man who was the Bully of humility.

A year or two younger than his eminently practical friend, Mr Bounderby looked older; his seven or eight and forty might have had the seven or eight added to it again, without surprising anybody. He had not much hair. One might have fancied he had talked it off; and that what was left, all standing up in disorder, was in that condition from being constantly blown about by his windy boastfulness.

Mr Bounderby

In the formal drawing-room of Stone Lodge, standing on the hearthrug, warming himself before the fire, Mr Bounderby delivered some observations to Mrs Gradgrind on the circumstance of its being his birthday. He stood before the fire, partly because it was a cool spring afternoon, though the sun shone; partly because the shade of Stone Lodge was always haunted by the ghost of damp mortar; partly because he thus took up a commanding position, from which to subdue Mrs Gradgrind.

'I hadn't a shoe to my foot. As to a stocking, I didn't know such a thing by name. I passed the day in a ditch, and the night in a pigsty. That's the way I spent my tenth birthday. Not that a ditch was new to me, for I was born in a ditch.'

Charles Dickens

Exercise 4: Hard Times

1 How old is Mr Bounderby from Extract 4?
2 What do you think the phrase 'metallic laugh' suggests about Mr Bounderby and his interests?
3 Choose four words or phrases from the passage which suggest that Mr Bounderby is a thoroughly unpleasant man. Explain as fully as you can how the expressions you have chosen suggest his unpleasantness.
4 Explain what is meant by 'the Bully of humility'.
5 Give one piece of evidence from the passage to show that Mr Bounderby is a bully.
6 Choose two descriptions that suggest that the writer is making fun of Mr Bounderby. Explain the reasons for your choice.

The final passage – Extract 5 – is by the Irish writer Flann O'Brien and describes a rather creepy old house.

Extract 5: *The Third Policeman*

I opened the iron gate and walked as softly as I could up the weed-tufted gravel drive. My mind was strangely empty. I felt no glow of pleasure and was unexcited at the prospect of becoming rich. I was occupied only with the mechanical task of finding a black box.

The front door was closed and set far back in a very deep porch. The wind and rain had whipped a coating of gritty dust against the panels and deep into the crack where the door opened, showing that it had been shut for years. Standing on a derelict flower-bed, I tried to push open the first window on the left. It yielded to my strength, raspingly and stubbornly. I clambered through the opening and found myself, not at once in a room, but crawling along the deepest window-ledge I had ever seen. After I had jumped noisily down upon the floor, I looked up and the open window seemed very far away and much too small to have admitted me.

The room where I found myself was thick with dust, musty and empty of all furniture. Spiders had erected great stretchings of their web about the fireplace. I made my way quickly to the hall, threw open the door of the room where the box was and paused on the threshold. It was a dark morning and the weather had stained the windows with blears of grey wash which kept the brightest part of the weak light from coming in. The far corner of the room was a blur of shadow. I had a sudden urge to have done with my task and be out of this house forever.

Flann O'Brien

Exercise 5: The Third Policeman

1 Where does the narrator of the story first land once he has climbed through the window?

2 What evidence can you find in the second paragraph that the house has 'been shut for years'?

3 Why is it difficult for the narrator to see into the far corner of the room in the final paragraph?

4 What evidence is there in the final paragraph that the inside of the house is deserted?

5 Choose five words or phrases that suggest to you that there is something mysterious about the house. Give reasons for your choices.

Reading for pleasure

Here are two more descriptions of places. The first one is another extract from *Hard Times* in which Dickens describes a fictional industrial town and makes it appear like a vision of hell. The second passage is an entirely different picture. It is an extract from another book by Gerald Durrell called *My Family and Other Animals.* In the passage he describes the appearance of a villa in which he and his family lived when he was a child growing up on the Greek island of Corfu. Read the two passages and think about how the writers achieve their effects – you may find this of help when you do the writing tasks on page 52.

Hard Times

It was a town of red brick, or of brick that would have been red if the smoke and ashes had allowed it; but as matters stood, it was a town of unnatural red and black like the painted face of a savage. It was a town of machinery and tall chimneys, out of which interminable serpents of smoke trailed themselves for ever and ever, and never got uncoiled. It had a black canal in it, and a river that ran purple with ill-smelling dye, and vast piles of building full of windows where there was a rattling and a trembling all day long, and where the piston of the steam-engine worked monotonously up and down, like the head of an elephant in a state of melancholy madness. It contained several large streets all very like one another, and many small streets still more like one another, inhabited by people equally like one another, who all went in and out at the same hours, with the same sound upon the same pavements, to do the same work, and to whom every day was the same as yesterday and tomorrow, and every year the counterpart of the last and the next.

You saw nothing in Coketown but what was severely workful. […] All the public inscriptions in the town were painted alike, in severe characters of black and white. The jail might have been the infirmary, the infirmary might have been the jail, the town-hall might have been either, or both, or anything else, for anything that appeared to the contrary in the graces of their construction.

Fact, fact, fact, everywhere in the material aspect of the town; fact, fact, fact, everywhere in the immaterial. The M'Choakumchild school was all fact, and the school of design was all fact, and the relations between master and man were all fact, and everything was fact between the lying-in hospital and the cemetery, and what you couldn't state in figures, or show to be purchaseable in the cheapest market and saleable in the dearest, was not, and never should be, world without end, Amen.

Charles Dickens

My Family and Other Animals

Halfway up the slope, guarded by a group of tall, slim, cypress-trees, nestled a small strawberry-pink villa, like some exotic fruit lying in the greenery. The cypress-trees undulated gently in the breeze, as if they were busily painting the sky a still brighter blue for our arrival.

The villa was small and square, standing in its tiny garden with an air of pink-faced determination. Its shutters had been faded by the sun to a delicate creamy-green, cracked and bubbled in places. The garden, surrounded by tall fuschia hedges, had the flower beds worked in complicated geometrical patterns, marked with smooth white stones. The white cobbled paths, scarcely as wide as a rake's head, wound laboriously round beds hardly larger than a big straw hat, beds in the shape of stars, half-moons, triangles, and circles all overgrown with a shaggy tangle of flowers run wild. Roses dropped petals that seemed as big and smooth as saucers, flame-red, moon-white, glossy, and unwrinkled; marigolds like broods of shaggy suns stood watching their parent's progress through the sky. In the low growth the pansies pushed their velvety, innocent faces through the leaves, and the violets drooped sorrowfully under their heart-shaped leaves. The bougainvillaea that sprawled luxuriously over the tiny iron balcony was hung, as though for a carnival, with its lantern-shaped magenta flowers. In the darkness of the fuschia-hedge a thousand ballerina-like blooms quivered expectantly. The warm air was thick with the scent of a hundred dying flowers, and full of the gentle, soothing whisper and murmur of insects.

Gerald Durrell

Writing

Similes

A **simile** is a figure of speech in which two things that are not obviously like each other are compared to make a description more vivid. A simile will often begin with a phrase introduced by *like* or *as*.

Here are some examples of similes taken from the passages on pages 47–48:

1 the piston of the steam-engine worked monotonously up and down, *like the head of an elephant in a state of melancholy madness*
2 a small strawberry-pink villa, *like some exotic fruit lying in the greenery*
3 the cypress-trees undulated gently in the breeze, *as if they were busily painting the sky*
4 roses dropped petals that seemed *as big and smooth as saucers*
5 marigolds *like broods of shaggy suns*
6 a thousand *ballerina-like blooms* quivered expectantly.

You'll notice that each of these similes (identified in *italics*) makes you think of the object it describes in an original way, bringing the object more clearly into your mind.

For example, the bright orange colour of the marigolds in number 5 and the shape of their petals are emphasised by the comparison with a 'shaggy sun'; and the comparison with large saucers in number 4 focuses on the size and perfection of the rose petals. In number 1 Dickens achieves many effects with his comparison of the movement of the steam-engine's piston with the movement of 'an elephant in a state of melancholy madness': he emphasises the unnatural and overwhelming size of the machines; he hints at the depressing effects they have on the lives of the workers; and he suggests the dangerous and potentially uncontrollable power and strength contained within them.

Metaphors

Metaphors are like concentrated similes. In a metaphor two dissimilar things are compared but rather than saying one is like the other, a metaphor goes a stage further and makes one thing become another.

For example, in the *Hard Times* passage on page 47, Dickens writes about 'tall chimneys, out of which interminable serpents of smoke trailed themselves for ever and ever, and never got uncoiled'. Here he is comparing the way smoke from factory chimneys appears in the sky to huge snakes floating in the air and coiling above the ground. However, rather than say 'the smoke was like

snakes' he gives the scene even more impact by making the smoke and the snakes the same thing. He succeeds in adding to the hellish portrait of the town. Metaphors are often used by poets who want to pack as much meaning as they can into as few words as possible.

A word of warning

Similes can be very effective aids in your imaginative writing; however, if a simile is used too often it tends to lose its effect. For example, the statement 'The young child was as good as gold' contains a simile ('as good as gold') but the comparison is so common that very few people when reading it think of the precious nature of gold and how this emphasises the value of the child's behaviour. Overused similes such as this are known as **clichés** and relying on them too much is a sign of lazy writing. Try to avoid doing this at all costs.

Another point to bear in mind when using similes is to make sure that there is always at least one point of comparison between the two objects in the clause and that the simile used is drawing attention to that quality in the first object.

Finally, remember that too many similes in the same paragraph can slow down your writing so it's usually better to use similes sparingly unless, as in Gerald Durrell's description of the strawberry-pink villa, you are trying deliberately to create a sense of peace and calm.

Exercise: Similes

Some overused similes are listed below. Think of some more original comparisons and then make up sentences in which they are used.

 1 clean as a whistle
 2 quiet as a mouse
 3 cool as a cucumber
 4 straight as an arrow
 5 as easy as pie
 6 like a bull in a china shop
 7 run like the wind
 8 hungry as a horse
 9 flat as a pancake
10 as cold as ice

Techniques for descriptive writing

Describing things effectively is an important way to directly involve your readers – the more convincing your descriptions, the more likely you are to draw your readers into your writing. It's important that you make your descriptions as clear as possible and you can do this by focusing on specific details of the person or place that you are describing.

An effective and straightforward way of including such detail is by concentrating on how what you are describing appeals to the different senses. Ask yourself the following questions before you start to write to help you focus on these details.

- What does the person or place look like?
- What sounds do I hear? (This could refer to a person's voice and/or movements, or to the sounds that are most apparent in the place you are writing about.)
- What does it feel like? (For example, you could describe a character's handshake or the feeling of damp and cold in a winter scene.)
- What does it taste like?
- What does it smell like?

Obviously, you may not want to include references to all the senses in every description – if you're describing your favourite pet it's unlikely that you will want to describe its taste!

Most importantly, good descriptive writing depends on choosing exactly the right word to communicate what is in your mind. It's usually better to present your description in a dynamic way through an effective choice of verbs and adverbs, rather than slowing down your description with too many adjectives and similes. Consider the following sentences.

- The teacher *came* into the classroom and *sat* on his chair behind the desk.
- The teacher *drifted* into the classroom and *slumped* into his chair behind the desk.
- The teacher *stormed* into the classroom and *positioned* himself on the chair behind his desk.

Each of these sentences conveys the same basic information (a teacher entered a classroom and sat at his desk). However, the different choice of verbs (in *italics*) in each sentence suggests a completely different account of events. The first one is neutral in what it tells us; the other two sentences are much more vivid and give a much clearer indication of the mood and character of the teacher.

Exercise: Developing a description

Here are some brief notes made by a writer as to what is to be included in a description of a scene.

Night time; house; trees; countryside; people entering house; cars; moonlight; noises in background; people talking; food being cooked; man in shadow of tree.

- Write two short paragraphs in which you develop these notes to produce a detailed and vivid description.
- Through choosing your words carefully, try to create a warm and welcoming atmosphere in one of the paragraphs and then a sinister and threatening atmosphere in your other paragraph.

Exercise: Character and place description

Write two longer paragraphs in which you:

1 Describe an unusual and eccentric character. (It may help to base this character on someone you know, but you can, of course, add or make up details. It doesn't have to be a human being – it could be a pet or another animal.)

2 Describe the place in which this character lives. You should concentrate on creating a description of a place which matches the eccentric nature of the character you have described in the previous paragraph.

Speaking and listening

Activity

Imagine that you have been witness to a minor crime and that you are helping the police with their enquiries by giving them a description of the person or persons involved. Give your description to your group – you should base it on someone you all know (although not necessarily a member of the group) – and ask them to see if they can guess who you are describing. Remember: you wouldn't know the criminal's name!

Key skills

Punctuation

Commas

Commas are one of the most commonly used pieces of punctuation and are key in allowing you to express yourself precisely. It's important that you understand when and where you should use them, and not just put them into your writing at random. Commas have four main uses which should become second nature to a confident writer.

1 To separate words or phrases in a list or series (except for the last two items which are usually joined by 'and'). For example: 'Polly's bag contained all her favourite things; in it there were coloured pencils, felt tipped pens, a small paintbox with brushes, drawing paper and a notebook for writing down ideas.'

2 To separate the name or title of a person being spoken to from the rest of the sentence. For example: 'Mummy, I'm feeling very tired and my back hurts,' said Polly.

3 To mark off words or phrases that follow a noun and which are parallel in meaning to it. This is known as being in apposition. For example: 'Barbara, Polly's mother, met some of her friends in the park.' The phrase 'Polly's mother' is in apposition to 'Barbara' as the two are the same person.

4 To separate words and phrases such as 'however', 'therefore', 'by the way', 'nevertheless', 'moreover', etc. that have been added into a sentence. For example: 'Polly was feeling tired; however, she knew that she had to finish the long walk.'

Exercise: Commas

Copy out the following passage and then insert commas where necessary.

Mrs Lee the Headteacher of Springfield Primary School was proud of her school. The students were hard-working punctual well-behaved and interested in their lessons. The classrooms were well-equipped with modern furniture new textbooks computers and interactive whiteboards. Moreover when she walked round on her daily inspection she knew that she would be welcomed into the classrooms by every teacher in the school. Only that morning she had entered the classroom of Mr Miah the Deputy Head. Straightaway all the children stood up and said 'Good morning Mrs Lee we are very pleased to see you.' Mr Miah however appeared to be a little confused by their greeting and Mrs Lee realised that it must have been something they had done without any prompting from him.

Non-fiction

Reading

Writing that informs and persuades

Non-fiction is the term we use to describe writing in which the content is presented as fact; this is as opposed to fiction which is the term we use to describe writing in which the content is made up by the writer (for example, as in novels or short stories).

Non-fiction writing takes many forms. In Chapter 1 we looked at some straightforward types of factual text and saw how it is usually presented in a way to communicate information clearly and quickly to a reader. In this chapter, however, we shall be looking at more complex forms of non-fiction writing in which it may not always be particularly easy to separate true facts from the writer's own point of view.

Fact and opinion

A **fact** is something which can be proved to have existed or to have happened; it is a truth.

An **opinion** is someone's personal view about something for which there is insufficient proof that it is true.

For example:

> In the 2008 Summer Olympic Games, the swimmer, Michael Phelps, won eight gold medals. Michael Phelps is the greatest athlete who has ever lived.

In the statement above, the first sentence is a **fact** – it can be proved by historical records that Phelps won eight medals. The second sentence, however, is an **opinion**. There is no question that Phelps is a great athlete, but there is no absolute standard by which his greatness can be measured and his talent as an athlete proved to be greater than any other athlete who has ever lived.

One of the key skills of reading is to ensure that you can distinguish between fact and opinion. Sometimes people who want to persuade us to share their views will attempt to present opinions as if they were fact. Look at the following advertisement for 'Soapy' washing powder:

Soapy washes whiter than all washing powders ➤ **EVER!** ◄

Despite the very positive tone of this advertisement which makes it sound true, it is, in fact, a statement that cannot be proved or justified. It is simply a claim made by the manufacturers of the soap powder. Read it again, but, in your head, put the words 'The manufacturer says that …' before the words of the advertisement and you'll notice the difference!

In the long run, it probably isn't of great importance that advertisements frequently set out to mislead their audience as most people will soon find out the truth once they've tried the product. However, on other occasions, for example, in political manifestoes, the presenting of opinions as facts can have much wider and more serious consequences. Training yourself to read non-fiction writing critically is a skill which will benefit you throughout life.

Now read the following website article on pages 55–56 carefully and answer the questions that follow on page 57.

Save the orang-utan

About the orang-utan

Orang-utans are a species of great ape found only in South East Asia on the islands of Borneo and Sumatra, although evidence of their existence has been found in Java, Vietnam and China. The gentle red ape demonstrates significant intelligence, with an ability to reason and think and is one of our closest relatives, sharing 97 per cent of the same DNA as humans.

Indigenous peoples of Indonesia and Malaysia call this ape 'Orang Hutan' literally translating into English as People of the Forest.

In times past, the people of the jungle would not kill them because they felt the orang-utan was simply a person hiding in the trees, trying to avoid having to go to work or become a slave.

Orang-utans are unique in the ape world. There are four kinds of great apes: gorillas, chimpanzees, bonobos and orang-utans. Only the orang-utan comes from Asia; the others all come from Africa. There are two separate

Orang-utan means People of the Forest

|||➡

species of orang-utan – the Sumatran orang-utan (*Pongo abelii*) and the Bornean orang-utan (*Pongo pygmaeus*). Orang-utans are only found on the islands of Sumatra and Borneo.

The orang-utan is the only strictly arboreal ape and is actually the largest tree living mammal in the world. The rest of the apes do climb and build sleeping nests in the trees, but are primarily terrestrial (spending their lives on the ground). Every night they fashion nests, in which they sleep, from branches and foliage. They are more solitary than the other apes, with males and females generally coming together only to mate. Even the hair colour of the orang-utan, a bright reddish brown, is unique in the ape world.

www.SaveTheOrang-utan.co.uk

The devastating effect of palm oil

A palm oil plantation

Orang-utans are being pushed to the brink. In the past decade alone, their numbers have fallen by up to half.

Probably the biggest threat is the loss of their natural habitat – due to industrial scale deforestation, forest fires, mining interests and conversion to palm oil plantations. **In the past 20 years, around 80% of suitable orang-utan habitat has disappeared**. And only a tiny 2% of what remains is legally protected.

The world's insatiable demand for palm oil is one major factor in the orang-utan's decline. And it is estimated that palm oil is present in more than half of the packaged supermarket products on sale in the UK today.

Grown sustainably, palm oil can provide vital livelihoods in an environmentally friendly way. But so far, too many manufacturers seem reluctant to pay the little extra for sustainably produced oil.

The huge demand is placing an unbearable strain on the remaining rainforests of the world – not least in Borneo. And, as the forests disappear, the orang-utan inches closer and closer to extinction.

Please help us act now to avoid disaster. The orang-utan **can** be saved.

Exercise 1: Save the orang-utan

1 From the first section of the article headed 'About the orang-utan' write down five facts that you have learnt about the orang-utan.

2 Explain what is meant by 'indigenous peoples'.

3 Why did people of previous times not kill orang-utans?

4 Find two details that make orang-utans 'unique in the ape world'.

5 Explain what is meant by 'arboreal'.

6 Using your own words, explain what has caused the numbers of the orang-utan to decline. Why, in particular, is the worldwide demand for palm oil causing so much of a problem?

7 What is meant by the word 'extinction'?

8 Put into your own words: 'Grown sustainably, palm oil can provide vital livelihoods in an environmentally friendly way.'

9 Compare the two sections in the article ('About the orang-utan' and 'The devastating effect of palm oil'). Are both sections equally factual or does one contain more opinion? Use evidence from the article in your response.

Emotive language

Emotive language is the term used to describe words chosen by a writer to influence readers by appealing to their emotions. This is mainly achieved through the way in which readers respond to the associations of the words used.

For example, a sentence such as: 'About one hundred students presented a petition to the Principal asking for a change to the school's homework policy.' conveys details of a specific event and the reader has a clear understanding of the facts. However, if the writer had written: 'A hundred-strong adolescent mob challenged the Principal by demanding a change to the school homework policy.' the changed wording would imply a much more confrontational episode, even though the basic facts are the same. In particular, think about how the use of the words 'hundred-strong adolescent mob challenged ... demanding' alter the reader's response when compared with the vocabulary used in the first sentence.

Newspapers in particular make great use of emotive language, both in their headlines and in their articles, in order to provoke their readers into supporting a certain point of view. It is a way of conveying opinions without making them obvious.

Now read the following articles over pages 58–61 taken from a newspaper website (the *Sun*); the first describes an establishment in Borneo where orang-utans are being trained to survive in the wild and the second article is by the journalist giving her view of her visit to the centre. Read them both carefully.

School where pupils monkey around

Published: 24 Apr 2010

His huge innocent eyes stare up mournfully

His habitat has been destroyed and his mother was left so disturbed after years in a tiny cage as a pet that she is unable to care for herself, let alone a baby.

Little Wigly has become an emblem of the urgent crisis facing Borneo's most famous resident, the orang-utan.

But amazingly, he is one of the lucky ones. At just three months old, he has not been so traumatised that he cannot learn the skills he will need to survive in the wild.

And his chances of being released into a safe area of the rainforest where he belongs look more hopeful than ever thanks to a ground-breaking project.

Wigly is being given 24-hour care at the Nyaru Menteng Centre in Kalimantan, run by the Borneo Orang-utan Survival (BOS) Foundation and made famous by Michaela Strachan and Steve Leonard in BBC1's *Orang-utan Diary*.

Furry nice to meet you … Wigly greets *Sun* girl Emma Cox

The tiny creature – whose face fronts a fundraising appeal for BOS – will need to stay at the centre for at least six years, mastering the skills he would have learnt from his mother in the wild, including finding food and avoiding predators.

But after that he may be one of hundreds of orang-utans BOS hopes to release in the biggest operation of its kind ever undertaken.

We can exclusively reveal that the charity has secured a piece of rainforest which will provide a safe environment for orang-utans ready to be released – 50 initially, with another 50 later this year, and potentially hundreds more to follow.

Dr Grainne McEntee, head of operations for BOS UK, says: 'These are exciting times for BOS, since this is the first set of truly rehabilitated orang-utans we have released from Nyaru Menteng.

'It signifies the culmination of events that we have been striving towards for the past ten years.'

The *Sun* visited Nyaru Menteng ahead of the planned release to see the work being done to reverse gloomy predictions that orang-utans may be extinct in the wild in as little as **FIVE** years.

There are 600 rescued apes here, with a further 400 at another nearby centre.

Once given a clean bill of health, the smallest newcomers such as Wigly are sent to Baby School, where they are given 24-hour care by trained local women called 'babysitters'.

Unable to suckle from mum, the orphans are given bottles of milk and tucked up in cots wearing nappies, their babysitters sleeping just yards away.

The orang-utans are unable to crawl or walk, so they are carried everywhere. Their babysitters soothe their whimpering by rocking them, just like a human newborn. Vulnerable though he looks right now, Wigly has the best chance of survival of any of the orang-utans, as he has never been mistreated and is young enough to adapt to forest life.

Sadly, others of his species can never leave. Adults which have been kept in cages for too many years will never learn the skills they need to survive on their own, while others are so disabled that they need constant supervision.

Current residents include a blind and lame baby, one with cataracts, and many adults simply too traumatised from their sad existence to ever recover.

But most will be released – particularly those found during their infancy when they are eager and able to learn.

After graduating from Baby School, the orang-utans go to Jungle School, where they are taken to the rainforests daily to learn the next stages of independence – how to climb

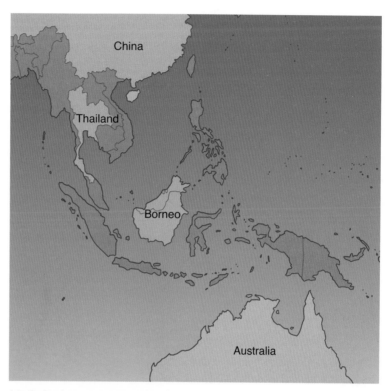

Into the jungle ... orang-utan centre is located in Central Kalimantan, Borneo

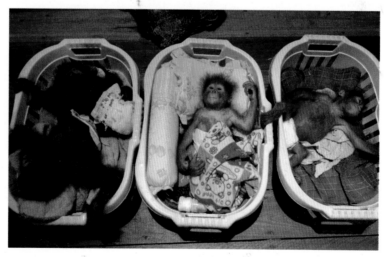

Snore of the jungle ... young orang-utans take a nap in their cribs

trees, socialise with other orang-utans, find termites to eat, and build nests of leaves in which to sleep and shelter from the frequent bursts of tropical rain.

After finally passing Jungle School, the orang-utans can go to Orang-utan University – one of five islands owned by BOS where they can live semi-wild, protected by security, monitored by staff, and fed twice a day from a distance until they are ready to return to the wild.

BOS will not release them until they are certain the land will **ALWAYS** be safe from poachers and loggers, and that there is enough food to sustain them.

But the charity has now secured an ideal area called Murung Raya – and if the initial release of 50 apes in July is successful, more will follow.

It is hoped that eventually the released apes will be totally self sufficient and could even begin breeding in the wild.

To find out how to help the orang-utans visit **www.savetheorang-utan.org.uk/thesun**

Hairy is … Wigly poses for cute baby shot

myView

BY EMMA COX
Senior Feature Writer

I WAS incredibly fortunate to be allowed into Nyaru Menteng.

A visit involved weeks of applying for permission then blood tests to prove I had no diseases I could pass to the orang-utans.

Once there, it was unforgettable. I met dozens of excitable orang-utans and was overwhelmed by the care they were given. Every morning they are released from their cages and they trot to school, some holding hands with their babysitters, eager ones rushing ahead, others trailing at the back.

They are as distinct from each other as humans, each with its own personality. But it is no wonder we are so fond of these apes – we share 97 per cent of their DNA, more than any other animal.

Looking into their eyes you can see their thought processes as they size you up. And their expressions – surprise, fear, contentment, even a mischievous sense of humour – are just like our own.

Holding hands with an orang-utan feels surprisingly like holding a child's.

The palm oil industry – it is used in hundreds of everyday products – means their habitat is being destroyed, leaving them starving and injured.

A hundred years ago there were 300,000 wild Bornean orang-utans. Today there are fewer than 40,000.

It costs £2,500 to release each rehabilitated orang-utan and monitor its progress. Wigly and his pals are counting on us.

How it works

Baby School
Babysitters feed apes milk and soothe their whimpering.

Jungle School
They receive rainforest training to help them climb trees, hunt termites, build nests, learn which fruits are good and how to flee snakes.

Orang-utan University
They live semi-wild on an island, monitored by staff and fed from a distance to assess if they are suitable for a return to the wild.

Exercise 2: The Nyaru Menteng Centre articles

1 The newspaper articles are written both to inform their readers and also to persuade them to sympathise with the plight of the orang-utans and perhaps to encourage them to join the campaign to help the animals. Now that you have read them, copy and complete a table like the one below and try to decide what is fact and what is the writer's opinion.

Fact	Opinion (and emotive language used)
The Nyaru Menteng Centre is in Kalimantan	The urgent crisis ('urgent' and 'crisis' are used to suggest that the situation is very serious and action must be taken now).

2 Look closely at the content of the articles, the vocabulary chosen by the writers (including the headline, subheadings and captions to the photographs) and the photographs themselves, and explain as fully as you can how the articles succeed in making readers aware of the problems facing orang-utans in Borneo and those who are trying to protect them.

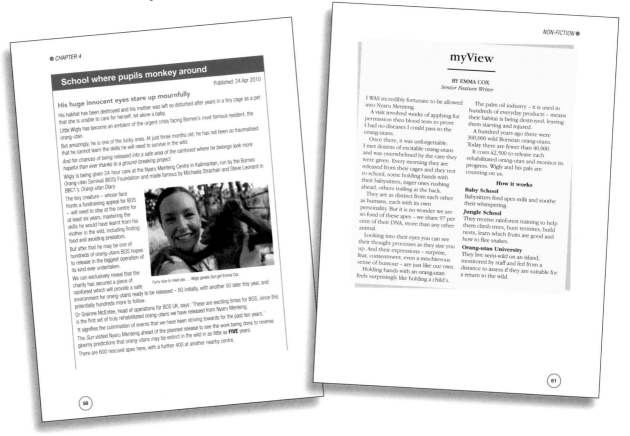

School where pupils monkey around
Published: 24 Apr 2010

His huge innocent eyes stare up mournfully

His habitat has been destroyed and his mother was left so disturbed after years in a tiny cage as a pet that she is unable to care for herself, let alone a baby.

Little Wigly has become an emblem of the urgent crisis facing Borneo's most famous resident, the orang-utan.

But amazingly, he is one of the lucky ones. At just three months old, he has not been so traumatised that he cannot learn the skills he will need to survive in the wild.

And his chances of being released into a safe area of the rainforest where he belongs look more hopeful than ever thanks to a ground-breaking project.

Wigly is being given 24-hour care at the Nyaru Menteng Centre in Kalimantan, run by the Borneo Orang-utan Survival (BOS) Foundation and made famous by Michaela Strachan and Steve Leonard in BBC1's *Orang-utan Diary*.

The tiny creature – whose face fronts a fundraising appeal for BOS – will need to stay at the centre for at least six years, mastering the skills he would have learnt from his mother in the wild, including finding food and avoiding predators.

But after that he may be one of hundreds of orang-utans BOS hopes to release in the biggest operation of its kind ever undertaken.

We can exclusively reveal that the charity has secured a piece of rainforest which will provide a safe environment for orang-utans ready to be released – 50 initially, with another 50 later this year, and potentially hundreds more to follow.

Dr Grainne McEntee, head of operations for BOS UK, says: 'These are exciting times for BOS, since this is the first set of truly rehabilitated orang-utans we have released from Nyaru Menteng.

'It signifies the culmination of events that we have been striving towards for the past ten years.'

The *Sun* visited Nyaru Menteng ahead of the planned release to see the work being done to reverse gloomy predictions that orang-utans may be extinct in the wild in as little as **FIVE** years.

There are 600 rescued apes here, with a further 400 at another nearby centre.

Furry nice to meet you ... Wigly greets Sun girl Emma Cox

myView

BY EMMA COX
Senior Feature Writer

I WAS incredibly fortunate to be allowed into Nyaru Menteng.

A visit involved weeks of applying for permission then blood tests to prove I had no diseases I could pass to the orang-utans.

Once there, it was unforgettable. I met dozens of excitable orang-utans and was overwhelmed by the care they were given. Every morning they are released from their cages and they trot to school, some holding hands with their babysitters, eager ones rushing ahead, others trailing at the back.

They are as distinct from each other as humans, each with its own personality. But it is no wonder we are so fond of these apes – we share 97 per cent of their DNA, more than any other animal.

Looking into their eyes you can see their thought processes as they size you up. And their expressions – surprise, fear, contentment, even a mischievous sense of humour – are just like our own.

Holding hands with an orang-utan feels surprisingly like holding a child's.

The palm oil industry – it is used in hundreds of everyday products – means their habitat is being destroyed, leaving them starving and injured.

A hundred years ago there were 300,000 wild Bornean orang-utans. Today there are fewer than 40,000.

It costs £2,500 to release each rehabilitated orang-utan and monitor its progress. Wigly and his pals are counting on us.

How it works

Baby School
Babysitters feed apes milk and soothe their whimpering.

Jungle School
They receive rainforest training to help them climb trees, hunt termites, build nests, learn which fruits are good and how to flee snakes.

Orang-utan University
They live semi-wild on an island, monitored by staff and fed from a distance to assess if they are suitable for a return to the wild.

Reading for pleasure

Here are two poems that draw attention to the Earth's endangered species.

'Or Will the Dreamer Wake?' – a poem about endangered species

Out in the East the jungle listens
The tigress, plaintive, growls in pain,
The great trees hear her breathing, shaking
Inside her still, the new lives wait.
These cubs could be the last ones ever
To freely live and roam and mate.
Our grandchild knows the tiger never
Or will the dreamer wake?

Far in the North the white bear snuffles
Down in her lair the gleaming snow
She waits for all the life she's making
Outside the crashing glaciers grow.
These cubs could be the last cubs ever
To freely live and roam and mate.
Our grandchild knows the white bear never
Or will the dreamer wake?

There in the West the song thrush warbles
She weaves her nest to hold her clutch
A long wait now to find a partner
The eggs are laid, there are not much.
These chicks could be the last ones ever
The last to fly and sing and mate.
Our grandchild knows the song thrush never
Or will the dreamer wake?

Deep in Ocean South the whale swims
Her song of birthing fills the seas
Thousands of creatures wait the moment
The solemn birth that they will see.
This child could sing the final whale song
The last to make the oceans shake.
Our grandchild never hears its mystery
Or will the dreamer wake?

Here in the centre, four directions gather
The path ahead leads up or down
Is this our last bright new world birthing?
Is this our waving as we drown?
This could be our last true moment
Knowing the truth, our choices make.
Our grandchild asks 'That was the moment!
And did the dreamer wake?

Medora Chevalier

'A Whale Song'

Amidst the ocean depths, far below the light,
A lone whale glides by in her watery flight.
A cry so lonely, a wailing of despair,
Something precious lost in the great somewhere.

Serene, yet watchful, moving always in fear
Of death's stillness, she searches ever near.
Pulling sunlight upward with care,
She caresses the surface and mists the salty air.

Nothing! Not a movement, except a hulking mass,
A predator's scent, a watchful, sweeping pass.
Dangerously taunting, the sight draws her near
As battered nets pull in Death and despair.

Her baby! Her angel! Death had claimed its song,
While a quiet stillness seemed to linger on.
Across the endless ocean, far below the sky,
A mournful mother sang a haunting lullaby.

Cheryl Kaye Tardif

Writing

From the articles you've read and analysed earlier in this chapter, you will have learnt that, as a writer yourself, it is important to have a clear idea of the purpose of what you are writing and an understanding of the audience for whom you are writing. In order to do this successfully you need to ensure that the **tone** of your writing (sometimes referred to as its **register**) is appropriate for your readers and matches the purpose of your text.

The tone of a piece of writing means simply whether it is funny, angry, informative, sarcastic, etc. A writer achieves tone by the vocabulary used – for example, emotive vocabulary for an article intended to arouse readers' feelings or impersonal vocabulary in a piece which is meant to do no more than provide factual information about something. The length and variety of sentences and paragraphs in a piece of writing also contribute to its overall tone.

The audience are the readers for whom the writing is mainly intended. The audience could be young children or university academics – good writers will ensure that they use a tone which is most suitable for their intended audience.

The following two activities give you the opportunity to practise writing in different tones.

Activity

- Choose a topic which means a lot to you and about which you have some knowledge. It could be a sport, a favourite pop group, a subject that you study in school or an issue about which you feel strongly such as protecting the environment.
- Write two articles of about 300 words each. One should be aimed at an audience of people of your age group and intended to give them basic information about your chosen topic. The second article should be aimed at people of your parents' age group. You should attempt to persuade them to become interested in your subject.
- Remember to adjust the tone of your writing to suit the audience and purpose.

Extended group activity

- Working in small groups of three or four decide on an issue which you all consider to be of importance to your country in today's world and produce a web-based campaign intended to educate (that is, to inform) people of your age in other countries about the issue.
- The campaign also needs to encourage them to care about the issue and to join you to promote it.
- The extract from the Tigers in Crisis website printed on pages 66–67 may give some help on how to write and design your website campaign but *you don't have to take endangered animals as your subject!*

The plight of tigers in crisis

Since 1900, the endangered tiger's habitat and numbers have been reduced by up to 95 per cent. Poachers continue to poison waterholes or set steel wire snares to kill tigers and tiger prey, selling their skins and body parts for use in traditional Chinese medicine.

The tiger is one of the most endangered species in the world

Despite 20 years of international conservation efforts, we are losing ground to save the tiger as, on the endangered species list, all sub-species of tigers are considered critically endangered species.

The crisis for tigers

The tiger, one of the most magnificent animals in the world, is also one of the most endangered species in the world. A cat of beauty, strength and majesty, the tiger is master of all and subject to none – except humans.

Of the eight original subspecies of tigers, three have become extinct within the last 60 years; and there are less than 50 South China tigers left on this planet – few, and possibly none, survive in the wild.

Tigers increasingly compete with expanding human population and industry for land and food, and many are killed by poachers who sell their skins and body parts as ingredients for traditional Chinese medicines. If these trends continue, the wild tiger may evolve from being an endangered species and off the endangered species list to become an extinct species.

A few of the remaining endangered subspecies may survive only in zoos; others will live only in stories, pictures and myths, never again to roam the earth.

Tiger body parts are sold for use in traditional Chinese medicine

Deep in the heart of Russia in late 1991, a large female Siberian tiger lay waiting in the wilderness beneath the dim silvery glare of a full moon rising up behind the clouds. The tiger was waiting for the opportunity to make a kill to feed her four growing cubs nearby in the brush.

The tiger did not know that she was being hunted, she was the prey. There was a poacher in the midst of her wilderness and before she would have a chance to feed or raise her young, her last cry could be heard throughout the forest. As the sun returned from beyond the horizon, the cubs ventured out to find their mother, only to discover her remnants scattered across the ground where she had once been.

The tiger, a critically endangered species, once lived in a vast region of wilderness that extended as far north as Siberia, as far south as the Indonesian island of Bali, as far west as Turkey, and as far east as the Russian and Chinese coasts. From icy cold mountains and forests to steamy, tropical jungles, the tiger species has adapted to a variety of terrain.

Unlike lions, leopards and cheetahs, tigers prefer to live in densely covered land where they can hide in tall grasses, camouflaged by their dark stripes, and ambush their prey.

Largest of all cats, tigers are formidable predators. With razor sharp claws, long teeth and powerful jaws and legs, tigers can bring down animals far heavier than themselves, including buffalo, deer and wild boar. The tiger's speed and refined hunting skills also capture feasts of small prey, contributing to the 40 to 100 pounds (18 to 45 kilograms) of meat that tigers can eat in a day.

The tigers

The Bengal tiger, or Royal Bengal tiger, roams a wide range of habitats including high altitudes, tropical and subtropical rainforests, mangroves and grasslands. They are primarily found in parts of India, Nepal, Bhutan, Bangladesh and Myanmar.

Indochinese tigers are located across southern China, Vietnam, Malaysia, Cambodia Laos, Thailand and eastern Burma. It is estimated fewer than 1500 Indochinese tigers are left in the wild. However, since the tiger has a very wide range, it makes it difficult for researchers to determine the exact numbers. Some scientists believe the numbers may be a few as 1200.

The Siberian tiger (or Amur-tiger) is considered a critically endangered species with the primary threats to its survival in the wild being poaching and habitat loss from intensive logging and development. It is estimated the wild population of Siberian tigers is around 350–450 tigers.

The South China tiger is the smallest of all the tiger subspecies, and it is the most critically endangered. Little is known about their exact numbers in the wild, but some estimates would put the number at under 20 tigers. Others would say that estimate is high. The reality is that no South China tiger has been seen in the wild for the last 20 years.

The Sumatran tiger is found only on the Indonesian island of Sumatra off the Malaysian Peninsula. Their habitat ranges from lowland forest to mountain forest and includes evergreen, swamp and tropical rainforests. It is estimated that only between 500 and 600 Sumatran tigers remain in the wild, and the actual number may be as low as 400. And their population is dwindling rapidly.

A Siberian tiger

Speaking and listening

Activity

As part of your website, you intend to include a five-minute video highlighting the key issues of your campaign. All group members will be part of this video. Present the content of the video as a group performance to the rest of your class.

Key skills

Vocabulary

Words that have similar meanings – such as 'happy' and 'joyful' – are called **synonyms**. However, it is unlikely that any two words have exactly the same meaning and can be used interchangeably in all contexts. For example, think about the slight difference in meaning between saying 'The children were happy on their way to school' and 'The children were joyful on their way to school'. Similarly, we can talk about something as being a 'happy coincidence' (which means that it was something *fortunate* that occurred) but a 'joyful coincidence' would suggest something different (that it was something that required celebration). Good writers are aware of the shades of meaning between synonyms and choosing the 'right' word is a key skill in creating effective emotive vocabulary.

Exercise: Synonyms

Write interesting sentences using each of the groups of words below, to show clearly their differences in meaning.

  1 Despondent, gloomy, heartbroken, sad, tearful.
  2 Assassinate, execute, kill, murder, slaughter.
  3 Excellent, faultless, glorious, perfect, pure.

Letter writing: Formal or business letters

One occasion in our everyday lives when we may have to write informatively is when we need to write a letter to an organisation or a business – for example, it may be to enquire about a job that is advertised or to complain about and ask for a replacement for something we have bought that doesn't work properly. Letters of this type are known as formal or business letters and there is a standard form in which they should be set out.

- Formal letters should begin with your address and the date on which you are writing in the top right-hand corner of the page.
- The title and address of the person to whom you are sending the letter then goes on the left-hand side of the page, starting below the line on which the date is written.
- The salutation (e.g. 'Dear Sir …') should be written directly under the last line of this address and, if it is necessary to quote a reference, this should be placed in the middle of the following line.
- You should finish your letter with either 'Yours sincerely' (if you have named the person you are writing to) or 'Yours faithfully' or 'Yours truly'.
- You then need to sign off the letter with both your first and family name.

As their name suggests, formal letters should not be too colloquial or chatty. They should be direct and to the point but the tone should be formal and polite. A formal letter should look like this.

```
                                              Your address
                                                     Date

Recipient's name
Recipient's address
Dear Mr _____

                    Ref: Groxyel 648292

_____
_____
_____
_____
_____

Yours sincerely
Geoffrey Chaucer
```

Exercise: Writing a formal letter

You have bought an item of electrical equipment which stopped working a day after you took it home. Write a formal letter to the manufacturers of the item in which you:

- state what the item is
- say where and when you bought it
- explain what appears to be wrong with it
- ask for a replacement item.

5 Folk tales

Reading

Folk tales are one of the earliest **genres** of story-telling. Many of them were originally made up centuries ago before writing and printing were in common use. The stories were handed down from generation to generation, usually in spoken form. Over the years, the different tellers of the original stories added their own details and adapted the stories to their particular listeners. Eventually, many of these traditional stories were collected into books by folklorists (people who study the traditions and culture of the past) and preserved for future readers.

In some parts of the world the tradition of telling stories **orally** still continues. Many of the original folk tales contain a moral or a lesson and many of these early stories still form the basis of the plots of more sophisticated stories and novels nowadays. Folklorists have found that many of the basic plots are common to more than one culture and can be found in the tales of countries from different continents.

A **genre** is a style or category of art, music, or literature. For example, the novel is a genre of literature and, for example, detective or science fiction stories are genres of the novel.

A story which is told **orally** is spoken out loud. 'The storyteller orally told the story of Jack and the Beanstalk. His audience listened with increasing excitement.' Stories which are part of the oral tradition usually contain quite a lot of repeated details and vocabulary. This is a deliberate attempt on the storyteller's part to make sure that the listeners can remember what has happened as they do not have printed copies of the story in which they can turn back a few pages to check details.

Here are two examples of folk tales from the Indian sub-continent – 'Stripes Tiger and the Boy' (pages 70–74) and 'Why the Sky is So High' (pages 75–76). Although the language has been updated, the stories themselves are traditional and very old. Read them both carefully and answer the questions that follow.

Extract 1: 'Stripes Tiger and the Boy'

Once upon a time, there lived a boy called Rahul in a village. One day, he was walking down a path when he came upon a large tiger trapped in a wooden cage. The villagers had caught him for stealing lambs.

'Hey mister!' cried the tiger as soon as he saw Rahul, 'I am so thirsty. Please open the cage so I can get a little drink. There is no water here.'

Rahul was frightened. 'But Stripes, if I let you out, you would jump on me and eat me up.'

'Never!' said Stripes looking suitably horrified. 'Whatever makes you think I would be so ungrateful? I just want a drink of water that's all. I won't take a minute, I promise,' he pleaded.

Rahul was a friendly boy. He opened the door and let the tiger out. The instant Stripes got out he sprang on the boy with the idea of eating him up.

'But Stripes,' cried Rahul, 'you promised you wouldn't. It is not fair for you to eat me when I set you free.'

'I kill prey for my food and it's perfectly right for me to eat you,' snarled Stripes, looking mean indeed. After much wailing by Rahul, Stripes agreed to ask the first three people who came along whether it was fair for him to eat up the boy or not.

The first to pass by was a donkey, Mr Bray. 'Mr Bray, Mr Bray, I set Stripes free from his cage. Now he wants to eat me. Is that fair?' asked Rahul.

Mr Bray looked up at Rahul tiredly and spoke out strongly. 'The farmer forces me to carry heavy loads on my back all day under the hot sun. Yet he doesn't feed me properly, and beats me with his stick. Even when I am sick, he expects me to work. Humans are an ungrateful race. Let Stripes eat you. It's one less person in the world.'

||||➡

Stripes licked his lips in anticipation. He collected some twigs and lit a fire and even put a pot on to boil. Seeing that Rahul got very frightened.

'Wh-wh-what is the pot for?' he asked with shaking knees.

'Heh, heh!' grinned Stripes, 'that's to cook and eat you now.'

'Wait, that's only one out of three people. We still have two more to ask,' cried Rahul frantically.

Stripes agreed. They wandered about and came to a place where an old horse was lying next to a heavily loaded cart. Rahul walked up to the horse and asked, 'Miss Mare! I just freed Stripes from his cage and now he wants to eat me. Is it fair?'

Miss Mare was barely able to get up. Her back was aching from dragging heavy loads.

She looked up and answered in a hoarse voice, 'There was a time when I was free to roam the forests. Then one day, my master captured me. He put a saddle on my back and a bridle in my mouth. He rode me hard. I have carried his children and grandchildren on my back. But now that I am old he makes me drag this cart.

'Today, when I couldn't pull it farther he left me without food or water to die here. Humans are very cruel. I say let Stripes eat you and that's the end of that.'

Rahul looked at Stripes and he saw Stripes sharpening his claws on a tree. He spoke rapidly, 'Okay this was my second chance. There is still one more left.'

Stripes grumbled and roared that he was hungry. He wanted Rahul to put an end to this foolishness. At last he reluctantly agreed to wait one last time.

Soon they saw a girl with a pail on her head walking down the road towards them.

Stripes called out to her. 'Dear child,' cooed Stripes, 'you are fair of face. I know you will be fair and just. Rahul freed me from a cage. But I am a tiger and I want to eat him. Can I or can't I?'

'Excuse me, what did you say?' asked the girl.

'He asked if it is fair for him to eat me when I have just set him free from his cage,' said a thoroughly dejected Rahul.

'Cage? What cage? I don't see any cage,' said the girl, looking all around. Her name was Preety.

'Yes, yes! A wooden cage,' cried Rahul anxiously, wringing his hands. 'Give us your opinion. Is it fair …'

'But how can I tell you when I haven't seen a cage around? I can't understand what the two of you are talking about at all!' said Preety.

'We are talking about the cage I was in,' explained an exasperated Stripes. 'You see ...'

'Exactly, I don't see at all,' said Preety, very sweetly. 'How can you "set him free", when he is already free?'

She turned towards Stripes. 'And how did you get into a cage, I want to know.'

'Grr,' said Stripes, gnashing his teeth. These humans are really dumb. He counted to 10 to avoid losing his temper. And then he began to explain.

'Last night I had come to the village to steal a lamb when I fell into a trap prepared by the villagers. They put me in a cage. This fool ...'

'Oh! What sort of cage was it and where was it?' interrupted Preety. 'I can't make head or tail of what you say.'

'A large strong wooden cage,' said Rahul.

'See here, I can't tell you without getting an idea of the cage,' said Preety. 'Why don't you two show me the cage? I will then give an answer in a second.' And so saying she winked at Stripes.

Stripes was love struck. Joyfully he took her small hand in his large paw and danced down the road towards the cage.

The unfortunate Rahul dragged his heels reluctantly.

At the cage Preety took over. 'Here Rahul, let's start at the beginning. Show me where you stood and where Mr Stripes was when you came along.'

'I was coming down this little path,' said Rahul.

'And Mr Stripes, you?' asked Preety.

'Here, inside the cage, of course,' replied Stripes.

'Oh, I would think this cage is not big enough for you, Mr Stripes. Won't you show me how you managed to stay in with your huge body?' asked Preety with an innocent look.

'See, I can get in and I was sitting here,' so saying Stripes leapt into the cage.

'Ahh! So that's where you were. But your paws can reach out. So why didn't you come out yourself?' asked Preety.

'I couldn't as the door was locked,' growled Stripes feeling quite uneasy at being back in the cage.

'Oh, excuse me,' said Preety looking suitably stupid. 'Being human I am very stupid. I can't imagine until you show me how. Will you show me how it works?'

Rahul pushed the door in. 'Like this.'

'And the lock?' asked Preety. 'Where is it?'

'Here!' cried Rahul. And he shut and bolted the door!

'Aha! So that's it,' said Preety clapping her hands. 'It does lock the door tightly.

'And now Rahul, as the door is locked, I suggest it stays locked. As for you, Mr Stripes, you have been very wicked and ungrateful. I hope you are locked up for a very long time.' Saying this, Preety took Rahul's arm and led him away.

B. Sumangal

Answer the questions below that relate to Extract 1.

Exercise 1: 'Stripes Tiger and the Boy'

1 Why had the villagers put Stripes into a cage?
2 Give the meaning of each of the following words or phrases as used in the passage:

> Stripes licked his lips in anticipation
> he reluctantly agreed
> a thoroughly dejected Rahul
> an exasperated Stripes
> gnashing his teeth

3 Using your own words as far as possible, explain why Mr Bray and Miss Mare did not care for humans.
4 Using your own words, explain as fully as you can the tactics used by Preety to trick Stripes back into the cage.
5 Describe Rahul's character and behaviour as fully as you can. Do you think he was wrong to let Stripes out of the cage in the first place?

Extract 2: 'Why the Sky is So High'

Long ago, the Sky was quite low. If you stood on a stool and stretched your hands up as high as they would go, you could touch the Sky.

At that time, far on the Horizon, where the Sky was always especially low, there was a village. In that village, in a little mud hut thatched with straw, there lived a bent Old Woman.

This bent Old Woman was the oldest woman in that village, possibly the oldest woman in the world. She was so old she no longer remembered any other way of being. She lived all alone in her little mud hut, for she had neither friend nor family left in this world. She had nowhere to go and no one to talk to. So all day long, she would potter round her hut, first cleaning this corner, now dusting that, now scrubbing this bit of floor, now sweeping that. The bent Old Woman thought of nothing else any more, except more and more ways of sweeping and scrubbing her little mud hut.

One hot summer, the land was dry with thirst. There was dust everywhere – on the trees, on the roofs of huts and houses, in people's throats and eyes, even in the air. All over the village people were coughing and sneezing and choking with the dust. Even the poor old Sky was not spared – it was so close to the ground that the slightest bit of wind would set it coughing with the dust that rose from the parched land.

The bent Old Woman's hut too was covered with dust. The Old Woman swept and swept and swept the little hut with her broom. She swept the inside of her hut, she swept the outside of her hut, she swept the front step and she swept the front yard. But the dust rose all around her in great brown clouds – the more she swept and plied her broom, the more the dust that rose from the earth.

The poor Sky began to choke with all the dust that the bent Old Woman was raising with her broom. The dust got into its throat and tickled its nose and made it sneeze – a great big sneeze that shook the world with its thunder. People covered their heads and ran indoors in fright. But the bent Old Woman barely noticed – she kept on sweeping with her broom.

The Sky sneezed again – the dust was becoming unbearable. It got into its eyes and made them water – so that great heavy drops of rain began falling into the dry dust below. The bent Old Woman barely noticed – till finally a big splodgy raindrop fell right on to the patch she had just swept.

The bent Old Woman glared at the Sky and scrubbed the splodgy raindrop away. But then another raindrop fell, and another, till her swept and scrubbed front step was blotchy with raindrops.

This was more than the bent Old Woman could bear. She stood up as straight as she could with her bent old back and shook her fist at the Sky yelling at it to stop raining on her nice clean front step. She cursed the Sky and threatened it, but the poor old Sky couldn't stop raining – its eyes were still so full of dust with all her sweeping.

At last, the bent Old Woman was so angry, that she picked up her broom, and thwacked the Sky with it.

The Sky gave another great sneeze and jumped out of her way. But the bent Old Woman kept thwacking it with her broom, again and again and again.

Finally the Sky could take it no more – the dust, the Old Woman's cursing, and especially her broom, thwacking it again and again and again. Sneezing and coughing, thundering and raining, the Sky flew up, up and away – out of reach of the Old Woman's broom and swore never to come down again.

So that is why the Sky is so high. Even on the Horizon, where it seems to be touching the earth, it really isn't any more.

Retold by Rohini Chowdhury

Now answer the following questions about Extract 2.

Exercise 2: 'Why the Sky is So High'

1 Where did the Old Woman live?
2 Give three details taken from the story about the Old Woman and the life she led.
3 Why was there so much dust?
4 What problems did the dust cause for the Sky and how did the Sky react to them?
5 Using your own words, describe how the Old Woman behaved towards the Sky.
6 According to the story, why is the Sky so high?

Now answer these questions about Extract 1 and Extract 2.

Exercise 3: Both extracts

1 What features of folk tales (repetition, etc.) do you find in these stories? How far do you think that they help readers to engage with the stories?
   (Note that the two stories use repetition in slightly different ways.)
2 Explain what you think might be the morals to these stories.

Ballads

Ballads are poems that tell stories. Many ballads were first composed hundreds of years ago and have features in common with folk tales. In some cases they tell of famous historical events such as battles that happened at the time. Like many folk tales, ballads were originally composed by unknown people and passed down through the generations in song before they were written down at a later period of time.

Here is an example of an early English ballad that was most probably first composed about 800 years ago although not written down until many centuries later. This is one of many ballads that tell of events in the life of the legendary outlaw hero, Robin Hood. In this story, Robin and one of his Merry Men, little John (so-called because he was very large in size), meet up with a pedlar (a travelling salesman). At first it looks as if the two outlaws are planning to rob the pedlar, but the story takes an unexpected twist. You'll notice that it also makes very effective use of repetition and, as in 'Stripes Tiger and the Boy', contains a lot of the main characters' direct speech which gives the story a dramatic and immediate effect.

'The Bold Pedlar and Robin Hood'

There chanced to be a Pedlar bold,
A Pedlar bold there chanced to be;
He put his pack all on his back,
And so merrily trudged over the lea.

By chance he met two troublesome men,
Two troublesome men they chanced to be,
The one of them was bold Robin Hood,
And the other was little John so free.

O Pedlar, Pedlar, what is in thy pack?
Come speedily and tell to me.
I've several suits of the gay green silks,
And silken bowstrings by two or three.

If you have several suits of the gay green silk,
And silken bowstrings two or three
Then, by my body, cries little John,
One half of your pack shall belong to me.

O nay, O nay, said the pedlar bold,
O nay, O nay, that can never be
For there's never a man from fair Nottingham,
Can take one half my pack from me.

Then the Pedlar he pulled off his pack,
And put it a little below his knee,
Saying, If you do move me one perch from
     this,
My pack and all shall gang with thee.

Then little John he drew his sword,
The Pedlar by his pack did stand,
They fought until they both did sweat,
Till he cried, Pedlar, pray hold your hand.

Then Robin Hood he was standing by,
And he did laugh most heartily,
Saying, I could find a man of smaller scale,
Could thrash the Pedlar and also thee.

Go you try, master, says little John,
Go you try, master, most speedily,
For by my body, says little John,
I am sure this night you will know me.

Then Robin Hood he drew his sword,
And the pedlar by his pack did stand;
They fought till the blood in streams did
     flow,
Till he cried, Pedlar, pray hold your hand.

O Pedlar, Pedlar, what is thy name?
Come speedily and tell to me.
Come, my name I ne'er will tell,
Till both your names you have told to me.

The one of us is bold Robin Hood,
And the other is little John so free.
Now, says the Pedlar, it lays to my good will,
Whether my name I choose to tell to thee.

I am Gamble Gold of the gay green woods,
And I travelled far beyond the sea,
For killing a man in my father's land,
And from my country was forced to flee.

If you are Gamble Gold of the gay green
     woods,
And travelled far beyond the sea,
You are my mother's own sister's son,
What nearer cousins can we be?

They sheathed their swords, with friendly
     words,
So merrily they did agree,
They went to a tavern and there they dined,
And cracked bottles most merrily.

Anonymous

The ballad form is still being used by song writers and poets as a way of telling a story through music. It provides a simple and direct form of narrative. Here is an example from the middle of the twentieth century; it is taken from a recording by the American folksinger Woody Guthrie and tells the story of another famous outlaw, Pretty Boy Floyd, an American bank robber of the 1930s.

'The Ballad of Pretty Boy Floyd'

If you'll gather 'round me, children,
A story I will tell
'Bout Pretty Boy Floyd, an outlaw,
Oklahoma knew him well.

It was in the town of Shawnee,
A Saturday afternoon,
His wife beside him in his wagon
As into town they rode.

There a deputy sheriff approached him
In a manner rather rude,
Vulgar words of anger,
An' his wife she overheard.

Pretty Boy grabbed a log chain,
And the deputy grabbed his gun;
In the fight that followed
He laid that deputy down.

Then he took to the trees and timber
To live a life of shame;
Every crime in Oklahoma
Was added to his name.

But a many a starving farmer
The same old story told
How the outlaw paid their mortgage
And saved their little homes.

Others tell you 'bout a stranger
That come to beg a meal,
Underneath his napkin
Left a thousand dollar bill.

It was in Oklahoma City,
It was on a Christmas Day,
There was a whole car load of groceries
Come with a note to say:

Well, you say that I'm an outlaw,
You say that I'm a thief.
Here's a Christmas dinner
For the families on relief.

Yes, as through this world I've wandered
I've seen lots of funny men;
Some will rob you with a six-gun,
And some with a fountain pen.

And as through your life you travel,
Yes, as through your life you roam,
You won't never see an outlaw
Drive a family from their home.

Woody Guthrie

Exercise 4: 'The Bold Pedlar and Robin Hood' and 'The Ballad of Pretty Boy Floyd'

1 Explain, using your own words, how Robin Hood and little John behaved towards the pedlar.

2 What was the name of the pedlar and why had he travelled far beyond the sea?

3 What do you learn about the characters of little John, Robin Hood and the pedlar from this ballad?

4 From 'The Ballad of Pretty Boy Floyd', why did Pretty Boy fight the deputy sheriff and what happened as a result of the fight?

5 Read the last two verses of 'The Ballad of Pretty Boy Floyd' carefully. What do you think the writer means by saying that some people will rob you 'with a fountain pen'? How does this comment and what the writer says in the final verse help you to understand the writer's attitude towards Pretty Boy Floyd?

6 Both ballads tell stories of characters who are lawbreakers but the writers appear to treat them as heroes rather than villains. By referring closely to the words of one or both of the ballads, explain as fully as you can how the writers succeed in presenting the characters as likeable people.

Reading for pleasure

Here is another folk tale; it is a story from Tibet.

'Plop!'

Many, many years ago there were six rabbits who lived on the shore of a lake, in a forest. One fine day, a big ripe fruit on one of the biggest trees fell down into the lake, making a loud 'plop!' when it hit the water. The rabbits were terrified, not knowing what this noise could be, and at once made off as fast as their four legs could carry them.

A fox saw them fleeing and called out, 'Why are you flying?'

The rabbits said, 'Plop is coming!'

When the fox heard this, he immediately started to flee with them. Next they ran into a monkey, who queried, 'Why are you in such a hurry?'

'Plop is coming!' replied the fox. So the monkey also joined in their flight.

Thus the news spread from mouth to mouth until a deer, a pig, a buffalo, a rhinoceros, an elephant, a black bear, a brown bear, a leopard, a tiger, and a lion were all running away, helter-skelter.

They had no thought at all, except to fly. The faster they ran, the more frightened they became.

At the foot of the hill there lived a lion with a great long mane. When he caught sight of the other lion running, he roared to him, 'Brother, you have claws and teeth, and you are the strongest of all animals. Why are you running like mad?'

'Plop is coming!' the running lion panted.

'Who's Plop? Where is he?' the lion with the long mane demanded.

'Well, I don't really know,' he faltered.

'Why make such a fuss then?' the long-maned lion went on. 'Let's find out what it is first. Who told you about it?'

'The tiger told me.'

The inquisitive lion with the long mane asked the tiger, who said that the leopard had told him, so the lion turned to the leopard, and the leopard answered that he had heard it from the brown bear. The question was passed on to the brown bear, who said he had heard it from the black bear. In this way, the black bear, the elephant, the rhinoceros, the buffalo, the pig, and the deer were all asked, one by one, and each of them said he was told by someone else.

Finally it came down to the fox's testimony, and he said, 'The rabbits told me.'

Then the lion went up to the rabbits, who squeaked in chorus, 'All six of us heard this terrible plop with our own ears. Come with us, we'll show you where we heard him.'

They led him to the forest, and pointing at it, they told the lion, 'The terrible plop is there.'

Just at this moment another big fruit fell from the tree and dropped into the water with a deep 'plop!'

The lion sneered.

'Now, look, all of you!' he said. 'You've all seen what that plop is. It's only the sound of a fruit dropping into the water. What is so terrifying about that? You almost ran your legs off!'

They breathed a sigh of relief. The panic was all for naught.

Writing

Now that you've read and thought about some folk tales and ballads, you could think about producing some of your own. Before you actually start to write, you might like to research some more examples, either from books in libraries or by searching on the internet. As a start you could try to look up some of the ballads that have been written about those famous outlaws: Robin Hood and Jesse James.

Activity

- Write your own folk tale or ballad (or both!). You could either make up your own story or write your own version of a traditional story that you have read.
- If you write your own story you could either produce a tale which contains a moral or you could choose to write about something of topical interest such as an important national or international news story (a major sporting event, for example) or something that has happened closer to home or within your school community.
- The choice of subject is really up to you. However, it's important that you should try to include as many of the traditional features of the style of the original tales or ballads (the use of repetition, refrains, direct speech, direct focus on the event, etc.) as you can in order to make yours sound authentic.
- Once the tales and ballads have been written they could be collected together into an anthology produced by your teaching group.

Techniques for writing

In 'Stripes Tiger and the Boy', much of the story is told through **direct speech**, which is when the words spoken by the characters are quoted exactly. When writing your own stories, you should include some passages of direct speech as it is an effective way of adding immediacy to your narrative. Also, if you're writing a story for an examination, it is a good way to show off your skills in using punctuation correctly.

However, in order to use direct speech effectively you should keep these points in mind:

- Be selective in your use of direct speech and remember that you should always use it to convey information, either about your story's plot or about your characters. Make sure your direct speech has a clear focus.

- Remember that, as the author of the story, you are in control of what your characters say. The skill is to make your characters' speech *sound* like everyday conversation. To do this effectively you will need to consciously shape it into a form rather than just randomly writing down a few colloquial phrases.

- You need to communicate a sense of your speakers' personalities through your use of direct speech. Remember that you don't need to stick to the rules of formal standard English when writing in direct speech – for example, it is fine to use abbreviations ('can't', 'won't', etc.) so that the speech doesn't sound stilted and unnatural. It is important, however, to remember your reader at all times. If your direct speech passages comprise nothing but teenage slang or attempts to represent the pronunciation of someone with a very broad dialect, they may be unintelligible to your readers.

- Too much direct speech can become boring and monotonous. Try to avoid this by varying the verb which introduces it (that is, don't always start with 'said') and vary the pattern of where the verb is placed (at the beginning of the speech, at the end of the speech, in the middle of the speech).

Here is an extract from the opening chapter of William Golding's novel *Lord of the Flies*. The book is about a group of schoolboys who have to survive on a tropical island after the plane they are travelling in crashes. Golding skilfully conveys important plot and character details through direct speech in the opening exchanges between two of the main characters. The two characters have just met each other after the crash.

Lord of the Flies

The fair boy was peering at the reef through screwed-up eyes.

'All them other kids,' the fat boy went on. 'Some of them must have got out. They must have, mustn't they?'

The fair boy began to pick his way as casually as possible toward the water. He tried to be offhand and not too obviously uninterested, but the fat boy hurried after him.

'Aren't there any grownups at all?'

'I don't think so.'

The fair boy said this solemnly; but then the delight of a realized ambition overcame him. In the middle of the scar he stood on his head and grinned at the reversed fat boy.

'No grownups!'

The fat boy thought for a moment.

'That pilot.'

The fair boy allowed his feet to come down and sat on the steamy earth.

'He must have flown off after he dropped us. He couldn't land there. Not in a plane with wheels.'

'We were attacked!'

'He'll be back alright.'

The fat boy shook his head.

'When we were coming down I looked through one of them windows. I saw the other part of the plane. There were flames coming out of it.'

He looked up and down the scar.

'And this is what the cabin done.'

The fair boy reached out and touched the jagged end of a trunk. For a moment he looked interested.

'What happened to it?' he asked. 'Where's it got to now?'

'That storm dragged it out to sea. It wasn't half dangerous with all them tree trunks falling. There must have been some kids still in it.'

He hesitated for a moment, and then spoke again.

'What's your name?'

'Ralph.'

William Golding

Speaking and listening

Activity

- Prepare a talk of about three to four minutes to give to your class or a small group in which you give information about someone (not necessarily someone famous) whose life deserves to be celebrated in a ballad.
- Explain why you think they deserve this honour and explain what qualities the ballad should focus on.
- The talk could, of course, be directly linked to work that you have done for the writing activity on page 82.

Key skills

Direct speech punctuation

When you use direct speech it is important that you punctuate carefully and correctly so that you don't confuse your readers. You should use speech marks (or inverted commas) to indicate passages of direct speech.
  There are four patterns by which speech can be shown.

1 Miss Mare looked up and answered in a hoarse voice, 'There was a time when I was free to roam the forests.'

2 'But Stripes,' cried Rahul, 'you promised you wouldn't. It is not fair for you to eat me when I set you free.'

3 'Yes, yes! A wooden cage,' cried Rahul anxiously, wringing his hands. 'Give us your opinion. Is it fair …'

4 'Here, inside the cage, of course,' replied Stripes.

Notes

- In number 1 a comma is used before the words spoken. The first word of the direct speech has a capital letter.
- In number 2 the words 'cried Rahul,' which break the direct speech, are separated from the rest of the sentence by commas. The opening word of the second part of this direct speech sentence does *not* have a capital letter, because it continues a sentence that has already started.
- In number 3 the two parts of the direct speech, separated by 'cried Rahul anxiously, wringing his hands.' are complete sentences. For this reason 'Give' has a capital letter.
- In number 4 the verb 'replied' comes after the actual words spoken; there is, therefore, a comma at the end of the direct speech before the following verb.

When you are writing a conversation between two or more people, remember that you should start a new line for each new speaker.
  Inverted commas are also sometimes used to indicate the titles of poems, short stories, books and films, etc. For example: 'The Owl and the Pussycat', 'Quantum of Solace'.

Exercise: Punctuating a conversation

- Write a conversation between two or three people in which you use the introductory verbs listed below in whatever order seems suitable. You can decide who the people are.
- Remember to punctuate your conversation correctly, to change the position of the verb of saying and to make sure that the verb you choose reflects the tone of what is being said:

  asked answered apologised begged muttered remarked
  retorted said snapped suggested

6 Short stories

Reading

We read stories for entertainment and enjoyment. To get the best out of what you read, it is important that you engage actively with the text and concentrate on what you are reading. To do this successfully you need two main skills. The first is to make sure that you understand as fully as you can what is happening in the story itself and are clear about the sequence of events. The second is to appreciate and understand what makes a particular story an effective piece of writing. This is a more complicated skill and is something that comes with experience of reading a range of fiction. It will help if you keep clearly in your mind the key features of any piece of fictional writing and then consider the way the writer presents them once you have finished the story.

Key features of fictional writing

Setting

The setting of a story is simply the place or places in which the events occur. It is important that the setting is convincing and in keeping with the type of story being written. When you write your own stories, you should try to ensure that the setting remains consistent as readers may become confused or lose interest if they do not find the setting credible – obviously, a fantasy story could be set in more bizarre surroundings than a story that attempts to capture the day-to-day life of students in a secondary school.

Characterisation

It is also important that readers should believe in the characters involved in the story so that they can sympathise and identify with some or all of them. The best way of achieving this is by making the characters consistent with the setting of the story. A bright green alien with five legs might well be convincing as a character in a story set in a faraway solar system. But such a character is not likely to be as convincing if it were to appear sitting next to you in a story very clearly set in your classroom at school!

Structure

The best stories are carefully planned and thought out before writing begins rather than being made up as the writer goes along. No matter what the length of a story is, the plot should show some development and contain a beginning, middle and end. It's possible, however, that these three elements of the story may not occur in such a straightforward order – some stories can be told very effectively by starting in the middle (or even at the end of events) and then using a flashback technique to show how this point was arrived at.

Language

It is through the words writers use that they make their characters and settings come to life, and allow them to establish a relationship with their readers. If they do not choose their words carefully and precisely, then there is a risk that the reader will be left with only a vague impression of what is being described and will be unable to engage fully with the story. This is especially important in short stories where writers must set the scene and introduce their characters quickly and effectively so that readers become immediately involved.

Now that you have some suggestions as to what to look for when reading a piece of fiction, it is time to look at an actual short story. The one that follows over pages 88–93 has been divided up into three sections with questions following each section. The questions will test your understanding of what you have read but also help you to appreciate the story as a whole and the writer's technique.

'Polly Helps a Friend' – Part 1

Polly pedalled her bicycle swiftly as Mother trotted alongside her. Mother had to hurry to keep up with Polly. They were on their way to the park for their weekly outing. Polly's big blue bag with pink pockets was slung over Mother's shoulder. It held many of Polly's favourite things that she used to create wonderful pictures that Mother would fasten to the refrigerator door for everyone to see. Wonderful things were a part of these trips, wonderful sunshine, wonderful breezes, wonderful colours and, most importantly, the big wonderful silver slide.

Polly was as happy as she could be today. The pink ribbon from her yellow pig-tails flew in the breeze behind her. Today, Polly felt more special than ever. Mother let her wear her new shorts outfit with the blue and pink flowers. Polly promised to be careful not to make it dirty. Polly loved Mother and always tried to make her proud. She wanted to be just like her when she grew up. Being outside today was like being in a beautiful dream of many colours. The windy sunshine was the yellowiest of yellows. It flooded Polly's smiling blue eyes and pink face as she looked at everything there was to see. [...]

Everything was wonderful today, even the birds sounded cheerier than ever. They whistled from nearby trees.

Polly's bicycle barely stopped as she jumped off. They had arrived at the special place in the park where the giant silver slide lived. Polly loved the slide; she got a shivery joy each time she slipped along its long slender back. She ran over to the slide.

'Slow down, Polly,' shouted her mother, smiling at her young daughter.

Barbara enjoyed these outings as much as Polly. She loved to just relax and visit with the other women she would meet there. They would trade stories about their children. When she felt like it, Barbara tucked her knitting or an interesting novel into Polly's bag. She felt a little tired from her brisk jaunt and plopped down at the nearest picnic table. Soon Carol, one of her friends, wandered over to her.

Polly watched her mother and the other woman. Polly liked it when her mother chatted or visited with other women. It gave her extra long playtime.

Susan A. Candela

Exercise 1: 'Polly Helps a Friend' – Part 1

1 What is Polly's mother's name?
2 What do you think Polly's favourite things are that are in the bag her mother is carrying?
3 Write down five details that you have learnt about Polly's appearance and the clothes she is wearing.
4 What three things does Polly's mother do to pass the time while Polly plays in the park?
5 Using your own words, explain why Polly is glad when her mother meets some friends.

6 Explain, using your own words, the following expressions from the text:
   a) 'They would trade stories about their children'
   b) 'her brisk jaunt'.

7 What do you understand by the phrase 'a shivery joy'? Why do you think Polly experiences this feeling?

8 Choose three words or phrases used by the writer that convey the idea that this was a special day and give reasons for why you have chosen them.

9 The writer repeats the word 'wonderful' many times in this opening section of the story. Why do you think she does this? Give reasons for your answer.

10 Give examples from the story of words and phrases that show that the writer is telling this story from Polly's point of view. Explain as fully as you can the effects achieved by this.

'Polly Helps a Friend' – Part 2

The slide was cold today, but this did not stop Polly from whisking down its bare back. The cold metal sent shivers of fun through her. Faster and faster she slid each time she climbed the endless steps. Up, up, up she went eager to swoosh along the cold, silver slide. Polly loved to daydream while she rode on the slide. She would close her eyes and think of herself as a lovely princess on a white horse. Some days, she would pretend that she was either a lost puppy or a lost kitten looking for its mother. She would crawl around while she meowed or whimpered sadly. Polly had heard her mother say that she had a good imagination. She wasn't really sure what this meant. She guessed that it meant that she was really great at pretending things.

Polly continued her trips up the stairs and down the slide. On what was maybe her twelfth trip, a strange sound shot into the air. It was a very painful groan. 'What's that?' she asked, jumping off the end of the slide.

'Oh, thank you!' came the answer over her shoulder.

'Who said that?' Polly asked again, looking round and round.

'I did.'

Polly bent at the waist, jumped to one foot and spun around. She was staring right at the slide. Two very, very sad eyes stared back at her. 'Thank you for getting off,' said a giant mouth just below the teary eyes.

'My back aches really badly today.'

Polly rubbed her eyes. Was this really happening? Could she believe her ears? Quickly, she looked over to where her mother sat with her friend. The two women were laughing and talking. Everything seemed okay. Polly looked back at the slide.

'Excuse me,' she said, 'did you speak to me?'

'Why yes I did,' answered the silver slide. 'I'm sorry if I startled you, but I can't take it anymore. Each and every day children jump on me and race down my back. It was fine when I was young, but I've grown so old and weary. I'm not nearly as strong and in the great shape I used to be. I love the children, especially you, Polly, but I shudder when they dig their feet into my back. What can I do? Can you help me, Polly?' With that, the poor old slide began to cry loudly. His steps shook with each large, wet tear. He pulled a large white handkerchief from his back step and blew his nose sadly. 'If this keeps up, I will have to be turned into a pile of steel and thrown onto the junk heap. I know all I need is a little rest. In time I will be okay. The park is putting in a new slide soon. Guess until then, I will have to be brave.'

Polly stepped back as she was puzzled. It took her long minutes to understand. This poor old slide that had given so many children so much fun over the years was asking her for help. She felt sad and important all at once.

'I'm sooooo sorry you are feeling bad,' she heard her small voice say. Her tiny hand gently patted the aching steel. 'There must be something I can do.' Polly thought and thought for some time. She walked to a swing and started to sit down, but stopped. She then started to go to her mother for help, but again stopped. 'Would Mother believe me?' Polly wondered aloud. 'A talking slide?' Polly did not know what to do to help her friend.

Susan A. Candela

Exercise 2: 'Polly Helps a Friend' – Part 2

1 Why do you think that the steps of the slide are described as 'endless'?
2 Choose two details from the first paragraph of this section and explain how they show that Polly has a good imagination.
3 What is it in particular that the slide says makes his back hurt?
4 Polly does not appear to be frightened when the slide speaks to her. Why do you think this is? (You should consider the description of the slide to help with your answer.)
5 Why do you think that Polly feels both 'sad' and 'important'?
6 What impression does the writer achieve by the statement, 'she heard her small voice say'?
7 Why doesn't Polly tell her mother about the slide?
8 Choose three words or phrases from this section that give human qualities to the slide. Explain your reasons for choosing them.
9 Polly has a good imagination. How does this detail help you to understand the way she reacts to the slide?
10 How does this section of the story help you to gain more of an understanding of Polly's character?

'Polly Helps a Friend' – Part 3

As she returned to the slide, Polly saw two workmen fixing one of the park benches. The workman dressed in grey coveralls nailed a brand new wooden arm to the bench. The second workman, who wore a white cap, took brushes and two cans from the back of his truck. Polly watched. He dipped his brush in one can of paint and stroked the wooden arm. Polly saw the green paint go on the arm and cover the wood. It looked new and shiny. People would have to wait a couple of days to sit on that bench she thought.

Suddenly her face lit up. She raced to her bicycle. 'I've got it,' she yelled. She grabbed for her big blue bag that was slung over the handlebars of her bicycle. Quickly, she sifted through it. She loved this bag; it had all of her favourite things. Polly pulled out a big, fat red crayon. She then snatched up a yellow sheet of drawing paper. Before a bird could eat a worm, she knelt and scribbled something on the paper. With that, she grabbed once more into the bag and was off in a race to her weary, waiting friend. 'I have just the thing,' she called to him, as she got nearer. The slide looked so unhappy. His big tears had made quite a large pool at his feet. Polly leaned over him. Her little hands worked quickly. She tucked and taped and finished. 'There,' she said, as she stepped back to see her work. Not too bad! This will work! Polly felt all warm and soft and good inside like she did when Mother hugged her. Just then she heard her mother's call that it was time to go home. 'Don't worry, now you can get the rest you need to feel better,' Polly called over her shoulder to the slide as she ran happily off to her mother.

Polly's arms waved to her mother. Barbara had been picking up the blue bag with its spilled crayons while she waited for her young happy daughter. She wondered why all the crayons were on the ground in such a hurried mess.

'What went on here?' she asked her daughter.

'A good thing,' answered Polly, hugging her mother. Polly felt proud and happy. Mother would have been proud of her too. Polly wanted to walk her bicycle home so she could think about her special day and how she had made the slide happy. She really had done a good thing.

Mother and daughter left the park, arms around each other. They passed a bench where a mother sat holding her young son. The little boy seemed very sad. He asked his mother, 'But, Mummy, why can't I go on the slide?'

Polly heard his mother's answer, 'You must stay off the slide for a few days, honey, the sign says "WET PAINT".'

Polly smiled her biggest smile and hugged Mother tighter.

Susan A. Candela

Exercise 3: 'Polly Helps a Friend' – Part 3

1 What two things do the workmen do to fix the park bench?
2 Why does Polly walk her bicycle home?
3 Explain clearly, using your own words, what Polly does to make the slide's life easier.
4 From your reading of the whole story, explain as fully as you can the relationship between Polly and her mother. Refer closely to details from the story in your answer.
5 Why is the fact that Polly is an imaginative child important to the story?
6 The park is described as an ordinary playground and Polly and her mother are normal people. How does the writer succeed in making the introduction of something unusual like a talking slide believable? In your answer you should consider carefully the language used to describe the slide and what it says and does.

7 Do you think the slide really speaks to Polly or is it just another example of her imagination? Give reasons for your answer. (There is no right or wrong answer to this question – if you like, you could give reasons for thinking either way.)

Poems that tell a story

Poems that tell stories are known as **narrative poems**. They have structures similar to those of novels and short stories and usually contain a range of characters. Narrative poetry is one of the earliest kinds of poetry and has links with such poetic forms as ballads (see Chapter 5, pages 77–79).

Some narrative poems are very long indeed and deal with grand themes – such as epic poems from Ancient Greek times by Homer. His *Iliad* and *The Odyssey* tell of the Siege of Troy and its aftermath. Other epic poems from earlier days include Virgil's *The Aeneid* written in Ancient Rome about a thousand years ago, the Anglo-Saxon heroic tale of *Beowulf*, John Milton's *Paradise Lost* written in England in the seventeenth century and Henry Longfellow's *The Song of Hiawatha* written in the United States about 200 years ago.

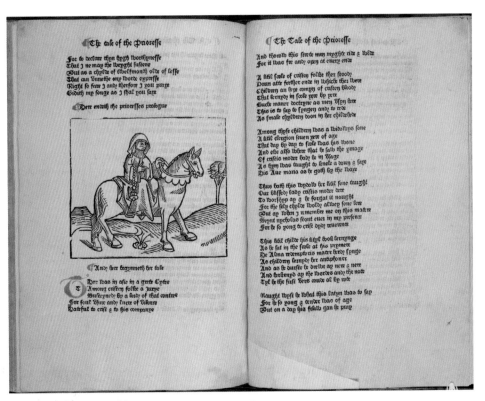

The Canterbury Tales by Geoffrey Chaucer

Apart from epic poems which deal with legendary heroic figures, there are other narrative poems which tell stories of the adventures of ordinary people. Again, many of these date from earlier times, such as Geoffrey Chaucer's collection of stories from the fourteenth century,

The Canterbury Tales, and the Scottish poet Robert Burns' 'Tam o' Shanter' from the late eighteenth century.

Many of these poems are over several thousand lines long. However, not all narrative poems are as long as this and not all deal with serious matters. There are two light-hearted examples of narrative poetry on pages 95–99: 'The Owl and the Pussycat' is a 'nonsense poem' written by Edward Lear in 1871; and 'Albert and the Lion' by Marriott Edgar tells the cautionary tale of an inquisitive boy and what can happen if parents don't keep a close eye on their children! Read and enjoy the two poems and then answer the questions that follow.

'The Owl and the Pussycat'

The Owl and the Pussycat went to sea
In a beautiful pea-green boat,
They took some honey, and plenty of money,
Wrapped up in a five pound-note.
The Owl looked up to the stars above,
And sang to a small guitar,
'O lovely Pussy! O Pussy, my love,
What a beautiful Pussy you are,
You are,
You are!
What a beautiful Pussy you are.'

Pussy said to the Owl, 'You elegant fowl,
How charmingly sweet you sing.
O let us be married, too long have we tarried,
But what shall we do for a ring?'
They sailed away for a year and a day,
To the land where the Bong-tree grows,
And there in the wood a Piggy-wig stood,
With a ring in the end of his nose,
His nose,
His nose!

'Dear Pig, are you willing, to sell for one shilling
Your ring?' Said the Piggy, 'I will.'
So they took it away, and were married next day,
By the Turkey who lives on the hill.
They dined on mince, and slices of quince,
Which they ate with a runcible spoon;
And hand in hand, on the edge of the sand,
They danced by the light of the moon,
The moon,
The moon!
They danced by the light of the moon.

Edward Lear

Exercise 4: 'The Owl and the Pussycat'

1 What did the Owl sing about in his song?
2 What detail tells you that the Pussycat liked what he sang?
3 Which word in the second verse tells you that the Pussycat thought that the Owl was handsome?
4 Why did the Pussycat fear that there might be a problem with their marriage?
5 How was this problem finally resolved?
6 What did they eat for their wedding meal?
7 Some of the words in 'The Owl and the Pussycat' are likely to be unfamiliar to you. Some of these are nonsense words, made up by the poet. Before checking to see if they are to be found in a dictionary, make up your own definitions for the words and then check to see if they really exist.
8 Re-read the poem and then choose three examples of what would appear to be 'nonsense'. Explain as fully as you can how the poet has successfully created a setting which makes it possible for them to be believable.

'Albert and the Lion'

There's a famous seaside place called Blackpool,
That's noted for fresh air and fun,
And Mr and Mrs Ramsbottom
Went there with young Albert, their son.

A grand little lad was young Albert,
All dressed in his best; quite a swell
With a stick with an 'orse's 'ead 'andle,
The finest that Woolworth's could sell.

They didn't think much of the Ocean:
The waves, they were fiddlin' and small,
There was no wrecks and nobody drownded,
Fact, nothing to laugh at at all.

So, seeking for further amusement,
They paid and went into the Zoo,
Where they'd Lions and Tigers and Camels,
And old ale and sandwiches too.

There were one great big Lion called Wallace;
His nose were all covered with scars –
He lay in a somnolent posture,
With the side of his face on the bars.

Now Albert had heard about Lions,
How they was ferocious and wild –
To see Wallace lying so peaceful,
Well, it didn't seem right to the child.

So straightway the brave little feller,
Not showing a morsel of fear,
Took his stick with its 'orse's 'ead 'andle
And pushed it in Wallace's ear.

You could see that the Lion didn't like it,
For giving a kind of a roll,
He pulled Albert inside the cage with 'im,
And swallowed the little lad 'ole.

Then Pa, who had seen the occurrence,
And didn't know what to do next,
Said 'Mother! Yon Lion's 'et Albert',
And Mother said 'Well, I am vexed!'

Then Mr and Mrs Ramsbottom –
Quite rightly, when all's said and done –
Complained to the Animal Keeper,
That the Lion had eaten their son.

The keeper was quite nice about it;
He said 'What a nasty mishap.
Are you sure that it's your boy he's eaten?'
Pa said 'Am I sure? There's his cap!'

The manager had to be sent for.
He came and he said 'What's to do?'
Pa said 'Yon Lion's 'et Albert,
'And 'im in his Sunday clothes, too.'

Then Mother said, 'Right's right, young feller;
I think it's a shame and a sin,
For a lion to go and eat Albert,
And after we've paid to come in.'

The manager wanted no trouble,
He took out his purse right away,
Saying 'How much to settle the matter?'
And Pa said 'What do you usually pay?'

But Mother had turned a bit awkward
When she thought where her Albert had gone.
She said 'No! someone's got to be summonsed' –
So that was decided upon.

Then off they went to the P'lice Station,
In front of the Magistrate chap;
They told 'im what happened to Albert,
And proved it by showing his cap.

The Magistrate gave his opinion
That no one was really to blame
And he said that he hoped the Ramsbottoms
Would have further sons to their name.

At that Mother got proper blazing,
'And thank you, sir, kindly,' said she.
'What waste all our lives raising children
To feed ruddy Lions? Not me!'

Marriott Edgar

Exercise 5: 'Albert and the Lion'

1 Explain, using your own words, why Mr and Mrs Ramsbottom were not impressed by the sea at Blackpool.
2 Explain what is meant by 'he lay in a somnolent posture'.
3 Why did Albert poke the lion with his stick?
4 Explain, using your own words, the meaning of the last two verses of the poem.
5 The poem uses several words and phrases (such as 'nobody drownded') which are not correct standard English. Find some more of these expressions, explain them and say how they add to your enjoyment of the poem.
6 If the events in the poem really happened we would consider them to be very sad and upsetting. By referring closely to the poem, explain how the poet makes the episode entertaining and funny. In particular, consider the description of the eating of Albert and how the parents and other people react to this.
7 Try to listen to a recording of the poem being read and then say how this helps your understanding of it.

Exercise 6: Considering both poems

1 Both poems are written in rhyming verse. Consider carefully how the rhymes (sometimes deliberately 'bad' rhymes such as 'mishap' and 'his cap') contribute to their overall effect.

2 Compare the two poems by looking at their settings, the characters they feature and the way the stories are structured. You should write about both their similarities and differences.

Reading for pleasure

Here is another short story and then a poem that tells a story (although in a slightly different way from the two on pages 95–99). The poem can be found on pages 105–109.

'The Dragon Rock'

This story begins with Once Upon A Time, because the best stories do, of course.

So, Once Upon A Time, and imagine if you can, a steep sided valley cluttered with giant, spiky green pine trees and thick, green grass that reaches to the top of your socks so that when you run, you have to bring your knees up high, like running through water. Wildflowers spread their sweet heady perfume along the gentle breezes and bees hum musically to themselves as they cheerily collect flower pollen.

People are very happy here and they work hard, keeping their houses spick and span and their children's faces clean.

This particular summer had been very hot and dry, making the lean farm dogs sleepy and still. Farmers whistled lazily to themselves and would stand and stare into the distance, trying to remember what it was that they were supposed to be doing. By two o'clock in the afternoon, the town would be in a haze of slumber, with grandmas nodding off over their knitting and farmers snoozing in the haystacks. It was very, very hot.

No matter how hot the day, however, the children would always play in the gentle, rolling meadows. With wide brimmed hats and skin slippery with sun oil, they chittered and chattered like sparrows, as they frolicked in their favourite spot.

Now, their favourite spot is very important to this story because in this particular spot is a large, long, scaly rock that looks amazingly similar to a sleeping dragon.

The children knew it was a dragon.

The grown-ups knew it was a dragon.

The dogs and cats and birds knew it was a dragon.

But nobody was scared because it never, ever moved.

The boys and girls would clamber all over it, poking sticks at it and hanging wet gumboots on its ears but it didn't mind in the least. The men folk would sometimes chop firewood on its zigzagged tail because it was just the right height and the Ladies' Weaving Group often spun sheep fleece on its spikes.

Often on a cool night, when the stars were twinkling brightly in a velvet sky and the children were peacefully asleep, the grown-ups would settle for the evening with a mug of steaming cocoa in a soft cushioned armchair. Then the stories about How The Dragon Got There began. Nobody knew for sure, there were many different versions depending on which family told the tale, but one thing that everybody agreed on, was this:

> In Times of Trouble
> The Dragon will Wake
> And Free the Village
> By making a Lake

This little poem was etched into everybody's minds and sometimes appeared on tea towels and grandma's embroidery.

The days went by slowly, quietly and most importantly, without any rain. There had been no rain in the valley for as long as the children could remember. The wells were starting to bring up muddy brown water and clothes had to be washed in yesterday's dishwater. The lawns had faded to a crisp biscuit colour and the flowers drooped their beautiful heads. Even the trees seemed to hang their branches like weary arms. The valley turned browner and drier and thirstier, every hot, baking day.

The townsfolk grew worried and would murmur to each other when passing with much shaking of heads and tut tuts. They would look upwards searching for rain clouds in the blue, clear sky, but none ever came.

'The tale of the Dragon cannot be true,' said old Mrs Greywhistle, the shopkeeper.

It hasn't moved an inch, I swear,' replied her customer, tapping an angry foot.

It was now too hot for the children to play out in the direct sun and they would gather under the shade of the trees, digging holes in the dust and snapping brittle twigs.

'The Dragon will help us soon,' said one child.

'He must do Something,' agreed another.

'I'm sure he will.'

They all nodded in agreement.

A week went by with no change, the people struggling along as best they could. Some were getting cross at the Dragon and would cast angry, sideways looks at it when passing. The villagers were becoming skinny eyed and sullen.

Meanwhile, the children had a plan.

Quickly and quietly, they moved invisibly around town, picking and plucking at the fading flowers. With outstretched arms and bouquets up to their chins, they rustled over to where the giant rock lay, as still as ever.

The boys and girls placed bunches of flowers around the Dragon in a big circle. They scattered petals around its head and over its nose, then danced around and around it, skipping and chanting the rhyme that they all knew so well.

> In Times of Trouble
> The Dragon Will Wake
> And Save the Village
> By making a Lake.

The searing heat made them dizzy and fuzzy and finally they all fell in a sprawling heap at the bottom of the mound. They looked up at the rock.

Nothing happened.

A dry wind lazily picked up some flower heads and swirled them around. The air was thick with pollen and perfume. A stony grey nostril twitched.

'I saw something,' cried the youngest boy.

They stared intently.

An ear swivelled like a periscope.

The ground began to rumble.

'Look out! Run! Run!'

The children scampered in all directions, shrieking and squealing, arms pumping with excitement.

The rumbling grew and grew.

The Dragon raised its sleepy head. It got onto its front feet and sat like a dog. It stood up and stretched, arching its long scaly back like a sleek tabby cat. It blinked and looked around with big kind, long lashed eyes.

And then its nostrils twitched and quivered again.

The older folk were alerted by the screams and shrieks. The ladies held up their long skirts to run and the men rolled their sleeves up and soon the whole town stood together in a tight huddle at the foot of the hill, staring up at the large beast with mouths held open.

'AHHHHH AAHHHHHHHHHH!!'

The noise erupted from the Dragon.

'AHHHHH AAHHHHHHHHHHHHHH!!'

The families gripped each other tighter and shut their eyes.

'AHHHHH CHOOOOOOOOOO!!'

The sneeze blasted from the Dragon like a rocket, throwing it back fifty paces, causing a whirlwind of dust and dirt.

'AHHHHH CHOOOOOOOOOOOOOO!!'

The second blast split open the dry earth, sending explosions of soil and tree roots high into the sky like missiles, and something else too …

The people heard the sound but couldn't recognise it at first for it had been such a long time since their ears had heard such tinkling melody. As their eyes widened in wonder, their smiles turned into grins and then yahoos and hoorahs.

(Water, cold, clear spring water, oozed, then trickled, then roared out of the hole, down the hillside and along the valley floor.)

The torrent knocked over a farmer's haystack, but he didn't care.

The river carried away the schoolteacher's bike shed but she cared not a jot. It even demolished the Ladies' Bowling Club changing rooms but they howled with laughter and slapped their thighs. When the flood sent pools of water out towards the golf course, filling up sixteen of the eighteen holes, the men just hooted and whistled and threw their caps up in the air.

What used to be a dirty, brown dust bowl, now gleamed and glistened in the sunlight, sending playful waves and ripples across the lake and inviting all to share.

'HMMMMM,' sighed the Dragon sleepily, and showing his perfect movie star teeth. 'Seeing as I'm awake …'

And he lumbered forward with surprising grace and style and disappeared into the cool dark water with a small wave of a claw and flick of his tail.

They never saw him again. Some say he went to Scotland …

After the families had restored and rebuilt the village, and set up sailing clubs for the children, and scuba diving for the grandparents, they erected a bandstand and monument in the spot where the Dragon used to lay. Every year to mark the occasion, they would bring garlands of flowers and herbs and arrange them in a big circle. The children would have the day off school, for it was known as 'Water Dragon Day' and wearing the dragon masks that they had been working on all week, would skip and clap and sing.

> The Dragon helped Us
> As We said He would Do
> Hooray for The Dragon
> Achoo, Achoo, ACHOOOO!

And that is the end of the story.

Ellena Ashley

'Chocolate Cake'

I love chocolate cake.
And when I was a boy
I loved it even more.

Sometimes we used to have it for tea
and Mum used to say,
'If there's any left over
you can have it to take to school
tomorrow to have at playtime.'
And the next day I would take it to school
wrapped up in tin foil
open it up at playtime
and sit in the corner of the playground
eating it,
you know how the icing on top
is all shiny and it cracks as you
bite into it,
and there's that other kind of icing in
the middle
and it sticks to your hands and you
can lick your fingers
and lick your lips
oh it's lovely.
yeah.

Anyway,
once we had this chocolate cake for tea
and later I went to bed
but while I was in bed
I found myself waking up
licking my lips
and smiling.
I woke up proper.
'The chocolate cake.'
It was the first thing
I thought of.

I could almost see it
so I thought,
what if I go downstairs
and have a little nibble, yeah?

It was all dark
everyone was in bed
so it must have been really late
but I got out of bed,
crept out of the door

there's always a creaky floorboard, isn't there?

Past Mum and Dad's room,
careful not to tread on bits of broken toys
or bits of Lego
you know what it's like treading on Lego
with your bare feet,

yowwww
shhhhhhh

downstairs
into the kitchen
open the cupboard
and there it is
all shining.

So I take it out of the cupboard
put it on the table
and I see that
there's a few crumbs lying about on the plate,
so I lick my finger and run my finger all over the crumbs
scooping them up
and put them into my mouth.

oooooooommmmmmmmm

nice.

Then
I look again
and on one side where it's been cut,
it's all crumbly.

So I take a knife
I think I'll just tidy that up a bit,
cut off the crumbly bits
scoop them all up
and into the mouth

oooooommm mmmm
nice.

Look at the cake again.

That looks a bit funny now,
one side doesn't match the other
I'll just even it up a bit, eh?

Take the knife
and slice.
This time the knife makes a little cracky noise
as it goes through that hard icing on top.

A whole slice this time,

into the mouth.

Oh the icing on top
and the icing in the middle
ohhhhhh oooo mmmmmm.

But now
I can't stop myself
Knife –
I just take any old slice at it
and I've got this great big chunk
and I'm cramming it in
what a greedy pig
but it's so nice,

and there's another
and another and I'm squealing and I'm smacking my lips
and I'm stuffing myself with it
and
before I know
I've eaten the lot.
The whole lot.

I look at the plate.
It's all gone.

Oh no
they're bound to notice, aren't they,
a whole chocolate cake doesn't just disappear
does it?

What shall I do?

I know. I'll wash the plate up,
and the knife

and put them away and maybe no one
will notice, eh?

So I do that
and creep creep creep
back to bed
into bed
doze off
licking my lips
with a lovely feeling in my belly.
Mmmmmmmmmm.

In the morning I get up,
downstairs,
have breakfast,
Mum's saying,
'Have you got your dinner money?'
and I say,
'Yes.'
'And don't forget to take some chocolate cake with you.'
I stopped breathing.

'What's the matter,' she says,
'you normally jump at chocolate cake?'

I'm still not breathing,
and she's looking at me very closely now.

She's looking at me just below my mouth.
'What's that?' she says.
'What's what?' I say.

'What's that there?'
'Where?'
'There,' she says, pointing at my chin.
'I don't know,' I say.
'It looks like chocolate,' she says.
'It's not chocolate is it?'
No answer.
'Is it?'
'I don't know.'
She goes to the cupboard
looks in, up, top, middle, bottom,
turns back to me.
'It's gone.
It's gone.
You haven't eaten it, have you?'
'I don't know.'
'You don't know. You don't know if you've eaten a whole
chocolate cake or not?
When? When did you eat it?'

So I told her,

and she said
well what could she say?
'That's the last time I give you any cake to take
to school.
Now go. Get out
no wait
not before you've washed your dirty sticky face.'
I went upstairs
looked in the mirror
and there it was,
just below my mouth,
a chocolate smudge.
The give-away.
Maybe she'll forget about it by next week.

Michael Rosen

Writing

Tips for planning your short story

- First of all decide on the main content feature of your story. It is a good idea to base your story on some form of conflict to provide narrative interest. The conflict could be between two people or two groups of people, or between a person (or persons) and their surroundings, or even involve one person trying to resolve his or her own conflicting wishes. Remember, however, that conflict does not necessarily involve violence and fighting! Some examples of conflict could include: a sporting contest; an attempt by someone to prevent the destruction of some open countryside to build a factory on; or, someone trying to resist the temptation to do something wrong despite pressure from 'friends'.

- Decide on a central figure (or protagonist) for your story. To make the story convincing, it will help if your central character has thoughts and feelings that you can share or empathise with.

- Decide whether you are going to tell the story using a first person or a third person narrator. If you decide to use a third person narrative (that is, by writing objectively using 'he', 'she', etc.) you will be able to show the thoughts and feelings of several characters. This is what is known as taking an omniscient approach. On the other hand, a first person narrative (using 'I') allows you to explore the thoughts and responses of the main character more fully but means that the events of the story are inevitably seen from that character's point of view.

- Decide on the setting for your story and try to keep it consistent throughout. It is a good idea to base the setting on somewhere that you know well as you will be able to use specific details that will make the story convincing to your readers.

- The main plot of your story will focus on the attempt or attempts of the main character(s) to face and overcome the conflict on which the story is based. Remember not to make the plot over-complicated – you are writing a short story not a novel and it is important that you engage your readers from the start and do not lose their interest.

Speaking and listening

> Group activity
>
> Working in small groups of three or four, create your own story that you will tell to your class. Together, decide on the skeleton structure of the story and divide it into three or four main episodes depending on how many people are in your group. Each member of the group then works on their own to produce an episode before you all get together again and tell the story, seeing how well the different episodes fit together. Finally, as a group, edit the account to make a final, polished version to tell your classmates.

Key skills

Punctuation

Commas

The main uses of commas are revised in Chapter 3 (page 53) if you need to recap on these before you look at some of the other uses of commas that follow. These other uses are not always straightforward and the rules are not quite as clear-cut. However, if you can master them, it will help you to make your writing more precise.

1 To separate a group of words beginning with a participle when a pause is needed as you read it: *The teacher, noticing that I was laughing, asked me what the joke was.*

2 To indicate the beginning of a passage of direct speech: *The teacher asked, 'Why are you laughing?'* (See Chapter 5, page 86, for direct speech punctuation advice.)

3 To break up a sentence into smaller parts to help make the meaning clearer for the reader: *The teacher, worried and upset, burst into the police station, rang the bell for attention and then, when the policeman on duty appeared, reported that his car had been stolen and used for a robbery.*

Exercise: Commas

Rewrite the following passage, inserting commas where necessary.

I remember that day very well. I took a message to Mr Lee my father's oldest friend. His house which is old and spooky was very close to where I lived. I walked along the path through his untidy overgrown weedy front garden and feeling a little uncertain not to mention slightly afraid I decided to knock on the door. Lifting the knocker I banged it hard on the door. The sound which echoed throughout the house seemed to hang in the air. There was no reply however so I tried again. The door finally creaked open; peering out at me as if it was a ghostly apparition was a withered bearded but kindly face. It said in a shaky voice 'Can I help you?'

Reading

In this chapter we shall look at some short stories and poetry written in various different parts of the world. They reflect the culture and life of people in a number of different countries. Some of these stories and poems were written originally in English; one of them, a story from Thailand, has been translated from the original Thai.

The first passage is an extract from a story by Amy Tan, who was born in America but comes from a Chinese family. In her story, 'Rules of the Game', she tells of a young Chinese girl living in America and developing her skills at playing chess. Much of the interest in the full story lies in the contrast between the attitudes of the people of her parents' generation – which are shaped by the Chinese culture in which they lived before emigrating to the United States – and those of Meimei, the girl telling the story, who was born in America and brought up there.

Amy Tan

Extract 1: 'Rules of the Game'

On a cold spring afternoon, while walking home from school, I detoured through the playground at the end of our alley. I saw a group of old men, two seated across a folding table playing a game of chess, others smoking pipes, eating peanuts and watching. I ran home and grabbed Vincent's chess set, which was bound in a cardboard box with rubber bands. I also carefully selected two prized rolls of sweets called Life Savers. I came back to the park and approached a man who was observing the game.

'Want to play?' I asked him. His face widened with surprise and he grinned as he looked at the box under my arm.

'Little sister, been a long time since I play with dolls,' he said, smiling benevolently. I quickly put the box down next to him on the bench and displayed my retort.

Lau Po, as he allowed me to call him, turned out to be a much better player than my brothers. I lost many games and many Life Savers. But over the weeks, with each diminishing roll of candies, I added new secrets. Lau Po gave me the names. The Double Attack from the East and West Shores. Throwing Stones on the Drowning Man. ||||➡

The Sudden Meeting of the Clan. The Surprise from the Sleeping Guard. The Humble Servant Who Kills the King. Sand in the Eyes of Advancing Forces. A Double Killing Without Blood.

There were also the fine points of chess etiquette.

Keep captured men in neat rows, as well-tended prisoners. Never announce 'Check' with vanity, lest someone with an unseen sword slit your throat. Never hurl pieces into the sandbox after you have lost a game, because then you must find them again, by yourself, after apologising to all around you. By the end of summer, Lau Po had taught me all he knew, and I had become a better chess player.

A small weekend crowd of Chinese people and tourists would gather as I played and defeated my opponents one by one. My mother would join the crowds during these outdoor exhibition games. She sat proudly on the bench, telling my admirers with proper Chinese humility, 'Is luck.'

A man who watched me play in the park suggested that my mother allow me to play in local chess tournaments. My mother smiled graciously, an answer that meant nothing. I desperately wanted to go, but bit back my tongue. I knew she would not let me play among strangers. So as we walked home I said in a small voice that I didn't want to play in the local tournament. They would have American rules. If I lost, I would bring shame on my family.

'Is shame you fall down nobody push you,' said my mother. During my first tournament, my mother sat with me in the front row as I waited for my turn. I frequently bounced my legs to unstick them from the cold metal seat of the folding chair. When my name was called, I leapt up. My mother unwrapped something in her lap. It was her *chang*, a small tablet of red jade which held the sun's fire.

'Is luck,' she whispered and tucked it into my dress pocket. I turned to my opponent, a fifteen-year-old boy from Oakland. He looked at me, wrinkling his nose.

As I began to play, the boy disappeared, the colour ran out of the room and I saw only my white pieces and his black ones waiting on the other side. A light wind began blowing past my ears. It whispered secrets only I could hear.

'Blow from the South,' it murmured. 'The wind leaves no trail.' I saw a clear path, the traps to avoid. The crowd rustled. 'Shhh! Shhh!' said the corners of the room. The wind blew stronger. 'Throw sand from the East to distract him distract him.' The knight came forward ready for the sacrifice. The wind hissed, louder and louder. 'Blow, blow, blow. He cannot see. He is blind now. Make him lean away from the wind so he is easier to knock down.'

'Check,' I said, as the wind roared with laughter. The wind died down to little puffs, my own breath.

My mother placed my first trophy next to a new plastic chess set that the neighbourhood Tao society had given to me. As she wiped each piece with a soft cloth, she said, 'Next time win more, lose less.'

'Ma, it's not how many pieces you lose,' I said. 'Sometimes you need to lose pieces to get ahead.'

'Better to lose less, see if you really need.'

At the next tournament, I won again, but it was my mother who wore the triumphant grin.

'Lost eight piece this time. Last time was eleven. What I tell you? Better off lose less!' I was annoyed, but I couldn't say anything.

Amy Tan

Answer these questions about Extract 1.

Exercise 1: 'Rules of the Game'

1 What do you think the old man (Lau Po) means when he says, 'Little sister, been a long time since I play with dolls'?

||||➡

2 Explain in your own words the meaning of 'benevolently'.

3 What do you think Meimei's reason was for taking the Life Savers with her and why do you think that she lost so many of them?

4 Explain using your own words the meaning of 'the fine points of chess etiquette'.

5 Why does Meimei think her mother will not allow her to play in the chess tournament?

6 Explain as fully as you can how Meimei managed to get her mother to approve of her playing in local chess tournaments.

7 What does the paragraph beginning, 'As I began to play, the boy disappeared ...' tell you about Meimei's state of mind when she is playing chess?

8 How does Meimei's account of the game show that she had learnt from Lau Po's teaching?

9 Explain carefully how what her mother says after Meimei had won the game shows that her mother does not fully understand how the game is played.

10 Looking at the passage as a whole, explain as fully as you can the mother's attitude towards her daughter's interest in playing chess.

The next passage comes from a story called 'The Gold-Legged Frog' by Khamsing Srinawk, who was born in what is now Thailand in 1930. This story tells us of the harsh life that the poor peasant families in the country endured during the early years of the last century.

Extract 2: 'The Gold-Legged Frog'

The sun blazed as if determined to burn every living thing in the broad fields to a crisp. Now and again the tall, straight, isolated sabang and shorea trees let go of some of their dirty yellow leaves. He sat exhausted against a tree trunk, his dark blue shirt wet with sweat. The expanse round him expressed total dryness. He stared at the tufts of dull grass and bits of straw spinning in a column to the sky. The whirlwind sucked brown earth up into the air casting a dark pall over everything. He recalled the old people had told him this was the portent of drought, want, disaster, and death, and he was afraid. He was now anxious to get home; he could already see the tips of the bamboo thickets surrounding the house far ahead like blades of grass. But he hesitated. A moment before reaching the shade of the tree he felt his ears buzz and his eyes blur and knew it meant giddiness and sunstroke. He looked at the soles of his feet blistered from the burning sandy ground and became indescribably angry – angry at the weather capable of such endless torture. In the morning the cold had pierced his bones, but now it was so hot he felt his head would break into pieces. As he recalled the biting cold of the morning, he thought again of his little son.

That very morning he and two of his small children went out into the dry paddy fields near the house to look for frogs for the morning meal. The air was chilly. The two children on either side of him shivered as they stopped to look for frogs hiding in the cracks of the parched earth. Each time they saw two bright eyes in a deep crack, they would shout, 'Pa, here's another one. Pa, this crack has two. Gold-legged ones! Hurry, Pa.'

He had hopped from place to place as the voices called him, prying up the dry clods with his hoe. He caught some of the frogs immediately, but a few jumped away as soon as he began digging. It was the children's job to give chase and pounce on them. Some they got. Some jumped into other fissures, obliging him to pry up a new cake of earth. Besides the frog, if his luck were good, he would unearth a land snail or razor clam waiting for the rains. He would take these as well.

The air had started to warm and already he had enough frogs to eat with the morning rice. The sound of drumming, the village chief's call for a meeting had sounded faintly from the village. Vague anger again spilled over as his thoughts returned to that moment. If only he had gone home then, the poor child would be all right now. It was really the last crack. As soon as he had poked it, the ground broke apart. A fully-grown gold-legged frog as big as a thumb leaped past the older child. The younger raced after it for about twelve yards when it dodged into a deep hoofprint of a water buffalo. The child groped for it. And then he was shocked almost senseless by the trembling cry of his boy. 'Pa, a snake, a snake bit my hand.'

A cobra spread its hood, hissing. When finally able to act, the father with all his strength had slammed the handle of his hoe three times down onto the back of the serpent, leaving its tail twitching. He carried his child and the basket of frogs home without forgetting to tell the other to drag the snake along as well.

On the way back his son had cried softly and moaned, beating his chest with his fists and complaining he could not breathe. At home, the father summoned all the faith healers and herbalists whose names he could think of and the turmoil began.

'Chop up a frog and put it on the wound,' a neighbour called out.

When another shouted, 'Give him the toasted liver of the snake to eat,' he hurriedly slit open the snake to look for the liver while his wife sat by crying. The later it got, the bigger the crowd grew. On hearing the news, all the neighbours attending the village chief's meeting joined the others. One of them told him he had to go to the district office in town that very day because the village chief told them the government was going to hand out money to those with five or more children, and he was one who had just five. It was a new shock.

'Can't you see my boy's gasping out his life? How can I go?' he cried resentfully.

'What difference will it make? You've called in a lot of doctors, all of them expert.'

'Go, you fool. It's two hundred baht they're giving. You've never had that much in your whole life. Two hundred!'

'Pardon my saying it,' another added, 'but if something should happen and the boy dies, you'd be out, that's all.'

'I won't go,' he yelled. 'My kid can't breathe and you tell me to go. Why can't they hand it out some other day? It's true I've never had two hundred baht since I was born, but I am not going. I am not going.'

'Jail,' another interjected. 'If you don't go you simply go to jail. Whoever disobeyed the authorities? If they decide to give, you have to take. If not, jail.'

The word 'jail' repeated like that unnerved him, but still he resisted.

'Whatever it is I am not going. I don't want it. How can I leave the kid when he's dying?' He raised his voice. 'No, I won't go.'

'You go. Don't go against the government. We're subjects.' He turned to find the village chief standing grimly at his side.

'If I don't go, will it really be jail?' he asked in a voice suddenly become hoarse.

'For sure,' the village chief replied sternly. 'Maybe for life.'

That did it. In a daze, he asked the faith healers and neighbours to take care of his son and left the house.

[*Nak goes to the meeting at the district office where, despite being humiliated by the official there, he is given the two hundred baht as he has five children. We pick up the story towards the end as he returns to his village.*]

The wind gusted again. The sabang and shorea trees threw off another lot of leaves. The spears of sunlight still dazzled him. The whirlwind still hummed in the middle of the empty rice field ahead. Nak left the shade of the tall tree and headed through the flaming afternoon sunshine towards his village.

'Hey, Nak …' The voice came from a group of neighbours passing in the opposite direction. Another topped it.

'You sure are lucky.' The words raised his spirits. He smiled a little before repeating expectantly, 'How am I lucky – in what way?'

'The two hundred baht. You got it, didn't you?'

'I got it. It's right here.' He patted his pocket.

'What luck. You sure have good luck, Nak. One more day and you'd have been out two hundred baht.'

Khamsing Srinawk

Answer these questions about Extract 2.

Exercise 2: 'The Gold-Legged Frog'

1 Read the first three paragraphs of the story very carefully and explain what makes Nak's life so hard. Refer closely to the text.
2 Why do you think that Nak tells his son to bring the dead snake home with them?
3 Explain the attitude of the villagers towards Nak and his concern for his son. Do you find their attitude surprising and what does it tell you about their lives?
4 What do you learn from this episode about the ways in which the authorities look upon the villagers?
5 Explain fully why the villager says that Nak is lucky when he returns to the village with the money. Do you find this a satisfactory ending to the story? Give your reasons.

Now we are going to look at a complete story written by Chinua Achebe, who is a Nigerian writer. In this story he describes what happens when Michael Obi, a headteacher with progressive and modern ideas, comes into conflict with the traditional beliefs and culture of the area in which his school is situated.

Chinua Achebe

Extract 3: 'Dead Men's Path'

Michael Obi's hopes were fulfilled much earlier than he had expected. He was appointed headmaster of Ndume Central School in January 1949. It had always been an unprogressive school, so the Mission authorities decided to send a young and energetic man to run it. Obi accepted this responsibility with enthusiasm. He had many wonderful ideas and this was an opportunity to put them into practice. He had had sound secondary school education which designated him a 'pivotal teacher' in the official records and set him apart from the other headmasters in the mission field. He was outspoken in his condemnation of the narrow views of these older and often less-educated ones.

'We shall make a good job of it, shan't we?' he asked his young wife when they first heard the joyful news of his promotion.

'We shall do our best,' she replied. 'We shall have such beautiful gardens and everything will be just modern and delightful …' […] She looked at him as he sat folded up in a chair. He was stoop-shouldered and looked frail. But he sometimes surprised people with sudden bursts of physical energy. In his present posture, however, all his bodily strength seemed to have retired behind his deep-set eyes, giving them an extraordinary power of penetration. He was only twenty-six, but looked thirty or more. On the whole, he was not unhandsome.

'A penny for your thoughts, Mike,' said Nancy after a while, imitating the woman's magazine she read.

'I was thinking what a grand opportunity we've got at last to show these people how a school should be run.' Ndume School was backward in every sense of the word. Mr Obi put his whole life into the work, and his wife hers too. He had two aims. A high standard of teaching was insisted upon, and the school compound was to be turned into a place of beauty. Nancy's dream-gardens came to life with the coming of the rains, and blossomed. Beautiful hibiscus and allamanda hedges in brilliant red and yellow marked out the carefully tended school compound from the rank neighbourhood bushes.

One evening as Obi was admiring his work he was scandalised to see an old woman from the village hobble right across the compound, through a marigold flower-bed and the hedges. On going up there he found faint signs of an almost disused path from the village across the school compound to the bush on the other side.

'It amazes me,' said Obi to one of his teachers who had been three years in the school, 'that you people allowed the villagers to make use of this footpath. It is simply incredible.'

'The path,' said the teacher apologetically, 'appears to be very important to them. Although it is hardly used, it connects the shrine with their place of burial.'

'And what has that got to do with the school?' asked the headmaster.

'Well, I don't know,' replied the other with a shrug of the shoulders. 'But I remember there was a big row some time ago when we attempted to close it.'

'That was some time ago. But it will not be used now,' said Obi as he walked away. 'What will the Government Education Officer think of this when he comes to inspect the school next week? The villagers might, for all I know, decide to use the schoolroom for a pagan ritual during the inspection.'

Heavy sticks were planted closely across the path at the two places where it entered and left the school premises. These were further strengthened with barbed wire.

Three days later the village priest or Ani called on the headmaster. He was an old man and walked with a slight stoop. He carried a stout walking-stick which he usually tapped on the floor, by way of emphasis, each time he made a new point in his argument.

'I have heard,' he said after the usual exchange of cordialities, 'that our ancestral footpath has recently been closed …'

'Yes,' replied Mr Obi. 'We cannot allow people to make a highway of our school compound.'

'Look here, my son,' said the priest bringing down his walking-stick, 'this path was here before you were born and before your father was born. The whole life of this village depends on it. Our dead relatives depart by it and our ancestors visit us by it. But most important, it is the path of children coming in to be born …'

Mr Obi listened with a satisfied smile on his face.

'The whole purpose of our school,' he said finally, 'is to eradicate just such beliefs as that. Dead men do not require footpaths. The whole idea is just fantastic. Our duty is to teach your children to laugh at such ideas.'

'What you say may be true,' replied the priest, 'but we follow the practices of our fathers. If you re-open the path we shall have nothing to quarrel about. What I always say is: let the hawk perch and let the eagle perch.' He rose to go.

'I am sorry,' said the young headmaster. 'But the school compound cannot be a thoroughfare. It is against our regulations. I would suggest your constructing another path, skirting our premises. We can even get our boys to help in building it. I don't suppose the ancestors will find the little detour too burdensome.'

'I have no more words to say,' said the old priest, already outside.

Two days later a young woman in the village died in childbed. A diviner was immediately consulted and he prescribed heavy sacrifices to propitiate ancestors insulted by the fence.

Obi woke up the next morning among the ruins of his work. The beautiful hedges were torn up not just near the path but right round the school, the flowers trampled to death and one of the school buildings pulled down … That day, the white Supervisor came to inspect the school and wrote a nasty report on the state of the premises but more seriously about the 'tribal war situation developing between the school and the village, arising in part from the misguided zeal of the new headmaster'.

Chinua Achebe

Exercise 3: 'Dead Men's Path'

Answer the questions below that relate to Extract 3.

1 Describe the character of Michael Obi and his wife Nancy and what you learn about their feelings, beliefs and attitudes.
2 Explain why Michael is so angry that the villagers are using the old path through the school grounds.
3 Explain the reasons that the village priest gives for why they should continue to use the path.
4 Explain what leads to the damage being caused to the school property.
5 Give your opinion as to whether Michael Obi was right to behave in the way he did or whether he should have respected the ancient beliefs of the village people.

Reading for pleasure

Here are two poems by writers from the Caribbean for you to enjoy.

'Nature'

We have neither Summer nor Winter
Neither Autumn nor Spring.

We have instead the days
When gold sun shines on the lush
green canefields – Magnificently.

The days when the rain beats like
bullets on the roofs
And there is no sound but the swish
of water in the gullies
And trees struggling in the high
Jamaica winds.

Also there are the days when the leaves fade from off guango trees
And the reaped canefields lie bare and fallow in the sun.
But best of all there are the days when the mango and the logwood blossom.
When the bushes are full of the sound of bees and the scent of honey,
When the tall grass sways and shivers to the slightest breath of air,
When the buttercups have paved the earth with yellow stars
And beauty comes suddenly and the rains have gone.

H.D. Carberry

'The Pawpaw'

Four little boys, tattered,
Fingers and faces splattered
With mud, had climbed

In the rain and caught

A pawpaw which they brought,
Like a bomb, to my house. I saw
Them coming: a serious, mumbling,
Tumbling bunch who stopped

At the steps in a hunch.
Releasing the fruit from the leaf

It was wrapped in, I watched them
Carefully wash the pawpaw

Like a nugget of gold. This done,
With rainwater, till it shone,

They climbed into the house

To present the present to me.

A mocking sign of the doom of all flesh
Or the purest gold in the kingdom?

Kamau Brathwaite

Writing

Letter writing: Informal or friendly letters

Although most of us keep in touch with our friends by email, texts, SMS messages or via social networking sites, we may still, at times, want to write something longer or more permanent. In cases like these we will almost certainly want to communicate using a letter. In Chapter 4 (pages 68–69) we looked at the conventions for writing formal or business letters. Now we're going to consider how to approach writing an informal or friendly letter – the type of letter you would write to a friend or relative who may live a long way away from you.

When writing a letter like this, it's important to remember a few important details. First, the person reading the letter will need to know where you live so that they know where to address any replies they send to you. Second, it's a good idea for you to let them know the date when you are writing and also for you to make it clear whom the letter is for. All of this information should be set out at the very beginning of the letter.

- Put your address at the top of the first page (it is conventional for it to be placed at the top right-hand corner).
- Straight after your address, put the date when you are writing.
- Below this, on a new line, on the left-hand side of the page, begin the letter with 'Dear …' followed by the first name of the person to whom you are writing.
- In a friendly letter, it's unlikely that you will use a person's title (Mr, Mrs, etc.) unless you are writing to someone who is in a position of authority or who works in an office that you need to contact. However, it is polite when writing to an older relative to begin with 'Dear Aunt or Uncle', for example. This opening of a letter is known as the salutation.
- After you have written the salutation, put a comma and then start the letter itself on the next line; it is conventional to begin with the first word of the actual letter immediately beneath the comma.
- Then write your letter, using paragraphs, etc.
- At the end of the letter, on a new line separate from the main body of your letter, end with what is known as the valediction followed by your signed name. The standard valediction for a friendly letter is 'Yours sincerely'. However, this ending may be too formal for a letter written to a close friend or relative and so it is perfectly acceptable to end with a valediction that indicates your closeness to the person to whom you are writing such as 'With love' or 'Yours affectionately'.

How informal your writing is will depend on your relationship to your letter recipient and how close you are to each other. For close friends, it is more than likely that you will want to write in a chatty, colloquial way. On the other hand, if you are writing a thank-you letter to your grandfather, your style will probably be a little more formal and correct.

Finally, it is also likely that in writing to a friend your letter may not always be well-structured as you go off at a tangent as things occur to you as you write – for example, asking about what other members of the family are doing. However, if you are required to write an informal letter as a class exercise or in response to an examination question, then you must ensure that it is well structured and makes sense to the teacher or examiner who will be reading it. In these circumstances, remember, the friend you are addressing is imaginary!

A personal letter will look something like this.

Your address

Date

Dear Lee,

      Sorry not to have written for such a long time but you'll never believe what's happened to me!

_____

_____

_____

_____

_____

_____

Must go now as Mum's telling me my tea's ready.

Lots of love,

Mandy

Activity

Write a letter to a friend who lives in a different country describing and explaining some of the traditions and customs of the country in which you live.

Speaking and listening

Activity

Give a talk to your class or group about the sort of things that you were scared of when you let your imagination run away with you when you were much younger.

Key skills

Structuring your writing

Paragraphs

A **paragraph** is a group of closely related sentences that develop a central idea. Writers give structure and organisation to their work by dividing a piece of continuous writing into paragraph units.

When you are planning your own writing, it is a good tip to plan your work by thinking about paragraphs and their topics.

All paragraphs should contain a **topic sentence** – this is a sentence that contains the main point of the paragraph. Although the topic sentence often comes at the start of a paragraph, you can vary the structure of your writing by changing the position of the topic sentence in different paragraphs. Once you have decided on your topic sentence, the rest of the paragraph should relate to it and develop from or towards it in a logical and coherent way.

Here is an example of a well-constructed paragraph which we looked at in Chapter 1. The topic sentence is written in bold type.

> **Volcanoes are not all alike**. Vesuvius is what is known as a composite volcano. Composite volcanoes have two different types of eruptions: the kind you see in the movies where the volcano spits molten lava and the kind where the volcano spews ash and rock. The eruption that destroyed Pompeii and Herculaneum was of the latter kind.

In this paragraph, the first sentence is the topic sentence – it introduces the point about the different types of volcanoes and the rest of the paragraph develops naturally from this point. Each new sentence then adds more details which provide the reader with further information.

Exercise: Sequencing a paragraph

The sentences below make up a paragraph, but they have been muddled up. Rewrite the paragraph, beginning with the topic sentence.

Playing proceeds by each player taking up as many matches as he or she wishes from any one pile.

Each player takes matches in turn.

A player may take all in the pile if he or she so desires.

Each pile can contain anywhere from ten to twenty matches.

Matchsticks is a game for two players.

The object of the game is to make your opponent pick up the last match.

Three piles of matches are placed upon the table.

Exercise: Topic sentences in paragraphs

Below are four topic sentences. Use each of them to write a single paragraph of your own. Try to vary the position of the topic sentence by putting one at the start of a paragraph, one in the middle and one at the end.

1 This is what I like best about my lessons at school.
2 When it was all over, she mounted her bicycle and rode away.
3 This is the main reason I enjoy visiting my grandparents.
4 When he came home, it was the first thing he remembered.

Reading

Throughout this book, we've looked at some poems as examples of different types of writing. Now, in this chapter, and in similar chapters in later books in the series, we will take a closer look at what poetry is and how it works.

One dictionary defines poetry as a 'composition in verse', which is a perfectly true factual description but most poetry enthusiasts would say that it doesn't really do justice to what poetry is. To come to a more satisfactory answer, we will think about the general characteristics of poetry and then look at some examples which illustrate them.

General characteristics of poetry

Poetry is one of the oldest forms of literature. The language of poetry is generally more concentrated than that found in other forms of writing (such as short stories or novels) as poets pack as much meaning as possible into the language choices they make. Poetry often makes use of rhyme and a regular rhythm which make it easy to remember. This was important because the earliest forms of poetry were passed on by word of mouth from generation to generation.

A fourteenth-century poem

In general, poets recreate experiences and feelings that we can all share and appreciate but use the power of their language to make these feelings and ideas fresh for us. The eighteenth-century poet Alexander Pope defined poetry as 'what oft was thought but ne'er so well expressed'. Another, later poet (Ezra Pound) described poets, like other artists, as being 'the antennae of a race'. Why do you think he chose this image?

Rhyme

Rhyme is when the endings of two or more words sound alike (for example, 'shore' and 'roar') and is a way of giving emphasis to words that carry important ideas. Using a regular pattern of rhyme also helps poets to structure and focus their thoughts. Although rhyme is an important feature of many poems, it is not something which is found in all poetry, and is not an essential requirement when you write your own poetry. Forcing rhyme into a poem can result in something which sounds very unnatural. However, experimenting with using different rhyming patterns is good training if you are keen to start writing your own poetry.

Rhythm and metre

Rhythm is another key feature of poetry. Everyone, when they speak, stresses some syllables and words more strongly than others – this is perfectly normal. For example, we pronounce the word '*an*imal' with the main stress on the first of its three syllables – try stressing either of the others and you'll hear how odd it sounds! In everyday speech, there is no specific pattern to the stressed and unstressed sounds that come out of our mouths. However, in many poems these stresses are organised into a regularly recurring **rhythm** in order to give the poem form and structure. A regular rhythmic pattern is known as the **metre** of a poem and is one of the main features which distinguishes poetry from prose – prose writing may well possess a rhythm but it doesn't usually have a metre.

There are many different types of metre used in poetry and you will soon become aware of them as you read a range of poetry. Much of the unique effect of poetry comes when poets combine a regular metre with a regular rhyming pattern.

Poetic devices

In order to focus as much meaning as they can into their poems, poets make use of figures of speech such as metaphors and similes (see Chapter 3, pages 49–50). Other literary devices commonly found in poems include **alliteration** and **onomatopoeia**. Alliteration is when words close together begin with the same consonant; for example, the '*s*nake *s*ipped with his long *s*low mouth, *s*ilently'. Onomatopoeia is when the sound of a word, such as 'crash', echoes its meaning.

When you are reading poetry it helps to read it aloud (or at least to imagine what it sounds like to be read aloud if, for example, you are on a crowded bus!). This will help you to appreciate how the different poetic devices the poet uses contribute to the overall effect of the poem.

Similarly, when you write about a poem you should try to explain *how* the different literary devices help the poet communicate his or her thoughts and feelings so you can show your teacher or the examiner that you have understood and appreciated what you have read.

Types of poetry

Although all poems are unique and all poets are individual, there are three main types (or forms) of poetry: **lyrical**, **narrative** and **dramatic**.

Lyrical poems are usually quite short and concentrated. Most lyrical poems are concerned with conveying strong feelings inspired by a particular experience – it could be love, or sadness or even the effect of listening to a bird singing. No matter what the stimulus is, the poet attempts to recreate and share it with their readers through the poem. Note that the word 'lyrical' comes from the old musical instrument called a 'lyre' and originally meant a poem that could be set to music.

A narrative poem is, as the name suggests, a poem that tells a story and we have already looked at some examples (see Chapter 6, pages 95–99). Narrative poems are usually quite long and the language used is generally less concentrated than that used in lyrical poems.

Dramatic poetry is the name given to the language used in some stage plays – for example, those of Shakespeare – in which the characters speak in verse, using metre and poetic language. The images created by metaphors in this poetic language can hint at ideas and meanings beyond the surface meaning of the words.

Reading different kinds of poems

Here are three poems for you to read, analyse and enjoy. The first two are humorous lyrical poems which, nevertheless, give you something to think about. In 'Warning', the poet Jenny Joseph looks forward to the way she hopes that she'll be able to behave when she grows old whereas Roger McGough in 'First Day at School' is looking back to childhood and writing about a child's experience of a first day at primary school.

The third poem is a narrative, written by the nineteenth-century poet Robert Browning. In this he captures the excitement of a thrilling horse ride as the narrator and his companions, Dirk and Joris, rush through parts of northern Europe to bring some unspecified good news from the town of Ghent in Belgium to Aix (modern day Aachen in Germany). The poem names the towns they ride through on their journey – when you've finished reading it, try to find a map of the area and follow their route on it.

Read the three poems carefully and answer the questions that follow each one.

'Warning'

When I am an old woman I shall wear purple
With a red hat which doesn't go, and doesn't suit me.
And I shall spend my pension on brandy and summer gloves
And satin sandals, and say we've no money for butter.
I shall sit down on the pavement when I'm tired
And gobble up samples in shops and press alarm bells
And run my stick along the public railings
And make up for the sobriety of my youth.
I shall go out in my slippers in the rain
And pick flowers in other people's gardens
And learn to spit.

You can wear terrible shirts and grow more fat
And eat three pounds of sausages at a go
Or only bread and pickle for a week
And hoard pens and pencils and beermats and things in boxes.

But now we must have clothes that keep us dry
And pay our rent and not swear in the street
And set a good example for the children.
We must have friends to dinner and read the papers.

But maybe I ought to practise a little now?
So people who know me are not too shocked and surprised
When suddenly I am old, and start to wear purple.

Jenny Joseph

Exercise 1: 'Warning'

1 Why do you think Jenny Joseph called her poem 'Warning'?
2 Explain in your own words some of the things that she plans to do when she grows old and why these are likely to shock people.
3 What is meant by the line 'And make up for the sobriety of my youth'?
4 Why does the narrator of the poem think that she ought to practise now?

'First Day at School'

A millionbillionwillion miles from home
Waiting for the bell to go. (To go where?)
Why are they all so big, other children?
So noisy? So much at home they
Must have been born in uniform
Lived all their lives in playgrounds
Spent the years inventing games
That don't let me in. Games
That are rough, that swallow you up.

And the railings.
All around, the railings.
Are they to keep out wolves and monsters?
Things that carry off and eat children?
Things you don't take sweets from?
Perhaps they're to stop us getting out
Running away from the lessins. Lessin.
What does a lessin look like?
Sounds small and slimy.
They keep them in the glassrooms.
Whole rooms made out of glass. Imagine.

I wish I could remember my name
Mummy said it would come in useful.
Like wellies. When there's puddles.
Yellowwellies. I wish she was here.
I think my name is sewn on somewhere
Perhaps the teacher will read it for me.
Tea-cher. The one who makes the tea.

Roger McGough

Exercise 2: 'First Day at School'

1 Choose three details mentioned by the child in 'First Day at School' which show that he finds the school strange and rather scary and explain why.

2 Why do you think the words 'To go where?' in Line 2 are put in brackets?

3 The child narrator is obviously confused by what is going on around him and misunderstands some of the words he hears. Quote some of these misunderstandings, explain them and say how they help you to understand his confusion.

4 What impression does the poem give you of the school? In particular, think about the reference to the railings.

Exercise 3: Comparing the poems

1 Think about the characters of the narrators of the two poems 'Warning' and 'First Day at School'. What similarities and differences can you find between them? You should refer to the poems in your answer.

2 Both poems are humorous. However, do you think they are making serious points? Give reasons for your answer.

Now read the Robert Browning poem below and answer the questions that follow. Some words printed in italics have been explained for you to the right of the poem.

'How They Brought The Good News From Ghent To Aix'

I sprang to the stirrup, and Joris, and he;	
I galloped, Dirck galloped, we galloped all three;	
'Good speed!' cried the watch, as the gate-bolts undrew;	
'Speed!' echoed the wall to us galloping through;	
Behind shut the *postern*, the lights sank to rest,	gate
And into the midnight we galloped *abreast*.	side by side
Not a word to each other; we kept the great pace	
Neck by neck, stride by stride, never changing our place;	
I turned in my saddle and made its girths tight,	
Then shortened each stirrup, and set the *pique* right,	the peak/pointed end
Rebuckled the cheek-strap, chained slacker the bit,	
Nor galloped less steadily Roland *a whit*.	a bit

'Twas moonset at starting; but while we drew near
Lokeren, the cocks crew and twilight dawned clear;
At Boom, a great yellow star came out to see;
At Duffeld,'twas morning as plain as could be;
And from Mecheln church-steeple we heard the half-chime,
So, Joris broke silence with, 'Yet there is time!'

At Aershot, up leaped of a sudden the sun,
And against him the cattle stood black every one,
To stare thro' the mist at us galloping past,
And I saw my stout galloper Roland at last,
With resolute shoulders, each butting away
The haze, as some bluff river headland its spray.

And his low head and crest, just one sharp ear bent back
For my voice, and the other pricked out on his track;
And one eye's black intelligence, – ever that glance
O'er its white edge at me, his own master, *askance*!   sideways
And the thick heavy *spume-flakes* which aye and anon   flakes of froth
His fierce lips shook upwards in galloping on.

By Hasselt, Dirck groaned; and cried Joris, 'Stay spur!
'Your Roos galloped bravely, the fault's not in her,
'We'll remember at Aix' – for one heard the quick wheeze
Of her chest, saw the stretched neck and staggering knees,
And sunk tail, and horrible heave of the flank,
As down on her *haunches* she shuddered and sank.   hindquarters

So, we were left galloping, Joris and I,
Past Looz and past Tongres, no cloud in the sky;
The broad sun above laughed a pitiless laugh,
'Neath our feet broke the brittle bright stubble like *chaff*;   husks of corn
Till over by Dalhem a dome-spire sprang white,
And 'Gallop,' gasped Joris, 'for Aix is in sight!'

'How they'll greet us!' – and all in a moment his roan
Rolled *neck and croup over*, lay dead as a stone;   head over heels
And there was my Roland to bear the whole weight
Of the news which alone could save Aix from her fate,
With his nostrils like pits full of blood to the brim,
And with circles of red for his eye-sockets' rim.

Then I cast loose my *buffcoat*, each holster let fall,   brownish-yellow leather coat
Shook off both my jack-boots, let go belt and all,
Stood up in the stirrup, leaned, patted his ear,
Called my Roland his pet-name, my horse without peer;
Clapped my hands, laughed and sang, any noise, bad or good,
Till at length into Aix Roland galloped and stood.

And all I remember is – friends flocking round
As I sat with his head 'twixt my knees on the ground;
And no voice but was praising this Roland of mine,
As I poured down his throat our last measure of wine,
Which (the *burgesses* voted by common consent)   citizens
Was no more than his due who brought good news from Ghent.

Robert Browning

Exercise 4: 'How They Brought The Good News From Ghent To Aix'

1 When did the horsemen set out on their ride?

2 List, in order, all the towns mentioned in the poem that they rode through.

3 Where were they when they first saw the sun?

4 Explain using your own words the lines:
'With resolute shoulders, each butting away
The haze, as some bluff river headland its spray.'

5 Choose two examples of the descriptions of the horses and explain how they convey the exhausting nature of the ride.

6 Explain using your own words the line: ''Neath our feet broke the brittle bright stubble like chaff'.

7 Choose two examples of alliteration used by the poet and explain how they help to bring the events of the poem alive.

8 By referring closely to the language used in the poem explain how the poet presents Roland as such a heroic horse.

9 How does the poem suggest the excitement of the ride? You should write about how the poet has used rhyme and rhythm to make his account come alive.

Writing

Exercise 5: Comparing two poems: 'Geography Lesson' and 'Black Beard'

The next two poems are both about schoolteachers and how they affect the children in their classes. Read both poems carefully. Write a comparison of the two poems in which you look at the ways in which they are similar and ways in which they are different. You should think about:

- what the teachers are like
- the effect the teachers have on their students
- what you learn about the teachers' own lives
- the words the poets use to create their pictures of the teachers
- how the rhymes help to emphasise key words
- what the poets think about their teachers.

To finish your comparison say what you like and dislike about each poem and say which one you prefer and why. *Remember to use the words of the poems to back up what you say about them.*

Copy and complete the following table as an aid for planning your comments.

	'The Geography Teacher'	Words used	'Black Beard'	Words used
What the teacher is like	Has dreams of travel	'spoke of lands he longed to visit'	Bad-tempered	'barks out' 'scowl' 'growl'
Effect on students				
Detail about the teacher's life				
Poet's opinion of the teacher				

'Geography Lesson'

Our teacher told us one day he would leave
And sail across a warm blue sea
To places he had only known from maps,
And all his life had longed to be.

The house he lived in was narrow and gray
But in his mind's eye he could see
Sweet-scented jasmine clambering up the walls,
And green leaves burning on an orange tree.

He spoke of the lands he longed to visit,
Where it was never drab or cold.
And I couldn't understand why he never left,
And shook off our school's stranglehold.

Then half-way through his final term
He took ill and he never returned,
And he never got to that place on the map
Where the green leaves of the orange trees burned.

The maps were pulled down from the class-room wall;
His name was forgotten, it faded away.
But a lesson he never knew he taught
Is with me to this day.

I travel to where the green leaves burn,
To where the ocean's glass-clear and blue,
To all those places my teacher taught me to love –
But which he never knew.

Brian Patten

'Black Beard'

He angrily barks out his orders.
His face wears a permanent scowl.
And if you should ask him a question
his only response is to growl.

His discipline methods are ruthless.
He believes in all work and no play.
And if you should happen to step out of line
It may be with your life you will pay.

I'd rather an octopus hug me.
I'd rather have sharks bite my rear
Than to walk into class on the first day of school
To find Black Beard's my teacher this year.

Robert Pottle

Speaking and listening

Group activity

Working in small groups of three or four, find two more poems that as a group you enjoy reading – you could choose other poems by some of the poets you've encountered in this chapter. Then, as a group, introduce your poems to the class, read them aloud (perhaps reading verses in turn) and explain what it is you like about them.

Reading for pleasure

Here are two poems about ghostly happenings for you to read and enjoy. Both poets were born in the nineteenth century but lived until the 1950s. Edna St Vincent Millay was born in Maine in the north-east of the United States and Walter de la Mare came from Kent in the south-east of England.

'The Little Ghost' by Edna St Vincent Millay is a gentle poem in which the poet shows sympathy and concern for the smiling ghost who visits her and who has 'no hint of sadness in her face'. Walter de la Mare's poem 'The Listeners', on the other hand, is much more mysterious – it appears to be an episode from a story about which we know no more. We don't know why the 'Traveller' has come to the deserted house, nor what his earlier promise had been. We don't even know who the 'Listeners' are, but these questions become unimportant – what matters is that we respond to the mysterious atmosphere that the poet has created.

'The Little Ghost'

I knew her for a little ghost
That in my garden walked;
The wall is high – higher than most –
And the green gate was locked.

And yet I did not think of that
Till after she was gone –
I knew her by the broad white hat,
All ruffled, she had on.

By the dear ruffles round her feet,
By her small hands that hung
In their lace mitts, austere and sweet,
Her gown's white folds among.

I watched to see if she would stay,
What she would do – and oh!
She looked as if she liked the way
I let my garden grow!

She bent above my favourite mint
With conscious garden grace,
She smiled and smiled – there was no hint
Of sadness in her face.

She held her gown on either side
To let her slippers show,
And up the walk she went with pride,
The way great ladies go.

And where the wall is built in new
And is of ivy bare
She paused – then opened and passed through
A gate that once was there.

Edna St. Vincent Millay

'The Listeners'

'Is there anybody there?' said the Traveller,
Knocking on the moonlit door;
And his horse in the silence champed the grass
Of the forest's ferny floor;
And a bird flew up out of the turret,
Above the Traveller's head:
And he smote upon the door again a second time;
'Is there anybody there?' he said.
But no one descended to the Traveller;
No head from the leaf-fringed sill
Leaned over and looked into his grey eyes,
Where he stood perplexed and still.
But only a host of phantom listeners
That dwelt in the lone house then
Stood listening in the quiet of the moonlight
To that voice from the world of men:
Stood thronging the faint moonbeams on the dark stair,
That goes down to the empty hall,
Hearkening in an air stirred and shaken
By the lonely Traveller's call.
And he felt in his heart their strangeness,
Their stillness answering his cry,
While his horse moved, cropping the dark turf,
'Neath the starred and leafy sky;
For he suddenly smote on the door, even
Louder, and lifted his head:–
'Tell them I came, and no one answered,
That I kept my word,' he said.
Never the least stir made the listeners,
Though every word he spake
Fell echoing through the shadowiness of the still house
From the one man left awake:
Ay, they heard his foot upon the stirrup,
And the sound of iron on stone,
And how the silence surged softly backward,
When the plunging hoofs were gone.

Walter de la Mare

Index